THE CALL OF THE ICE

THE CALL OF THE ICE

CLIMBING 8000-METER PEAKS IN WINTER

SIMONE MORO

foreword by **ED VIESTURS**

translated by **MONICA MENEGHETTI**

MOUNTAINEERS
BOOKS

Mountaineers Books is the publishing division of The Mountaineers, an organization founded in 1906 and dedicated to the exploration, preservation, and enjoyment of outdoor and wilderness areas.

MOUNTAINEERS BOOKS

1001 SW Klickitat Way, Suite 201 • Seattle, WA 98134 • 800.553.4453, www.mountaineersbooks.org

Original edition © 2012 RCS Libri S.p.A., Milan
La Voce del Ghiaccio
English-language translation copyright © 2014 by Monica Meneghetti

Printed in the United States of America
Distributed in the United Kingdom by Cordee, www.cordee.co.uk
17 16 15 14   1 2 3 4 5

Copy Editor: Julie Van Pelt
Design and Layout: Jen Grable
Front Cover photograph: *Simone Moro on Gasherbrum II* © Cory Richards/The North Face
Back Cover photograph: *Camp 1 on Gasherbrum II* © Cory Richards/The North Face
Photograph on page 221 by Marco Luzzani, www.marcoluzzani.com

A catalog record for this book is available at the Library of Congress

ISBN (paperback): 978-1-59485-903-8
ISBN (ebook): 978-1-59485-904-5

CONTENTS

FOREWORD

CLIMBING 8000-METER PEAKS IS ONE of the most physically difficult and mentally challenging endeavors that humans have ever attempted. Steep terrain. Hurricane-force winds. Subzero temperatures. Blinding snowstorms. Near impossibility of rescue. Constant discomfort. And the coup de grace—very little oxygen while dealing with all of these obstacles.

Yet mountaineers decided long ago that these challenges and difficulties are what make climbing these monstrous and isolated peaks so intriguing. People often ask me why I climb, and there's really no simple answer, other than perhaps the cliché, "If you have to ask, you'll never know." Climbers are willing to pay "the currency of toil" to reach a summit. We accept, and in some ways savor, discomfort, physical hardship, and a bit of mental stress.

But then there is Simone Moro. Not content with the normal challenges of climbing at 8000 meters, he chooses to amp up the difficulty meter to eleven: He climbs these peaks in winter, with shorter days, colder temperatures, and higher wind speeds.

Winter climbing in the Himalaya is relatively new. The first great achievement in that viciously cold season occurred in the winter of

1980 when members of a Polish team reached the summit of Everest. It was a large team comprising some of the strongest Himalayan superstars of the time. In traditional expedition style, utilizing siege tactics, the Poles methodically worked their way up the mountain, and although only two climbers—Leszek Cichy and Krzysztof Wielicki—reached the summit on February 17, it was a victory for the whole team. The pair radioed from the summit: *Strong wind blows all the time. It is unimaginably cold.* With the Polish flag flying from the summit of Everest on that bitter winter day, a new era of climbing had begun—one that Simone has embraced.

I met and climbed with Simone in Pakistan during the summer of 2003. My partner Frenchman JC LaFaille and I were hoping to climb both Nanga Parbat and Broad Peak during that season. Simone had the same ambition, and JC and I bought spots on Simone's permits. As it turned out, we would also share a base camp and work together on the mountain. Coincidentally, a very strong team from Kazakhstan was on the same schedule and we all spent many hours together in our communal dining tent sharing stories and jokes.

Simone made a terrific first impression: exuberant, affable, and considerate. He was no prima donna. He treated everyone, including our Pakistani staff and porters, with kindness and respect. Simone's team spoke Italian almost exclusively, but Simone spoke English quite well. Often, after telling a tale that left all of his teammates in stitches, he would retell it in English so that I, too, could appreciate the joke. And since we both had known Anatolij Boukreev, we discussed not only the tragic events on Everest in 1996, but also Simone and Anatolij's winter attempt of Annapurna in 1997 where Anatolij lost his life in an avalanche that Simone barely survived.

Simone joined JC and me on many of our forays up the mountain to fix ropes or carry loads. He moved with skill and grace over difficult terrain, always confident, always positive. Completely happy in the mountains, he clearly enjoyed the journey, and cared about more than the summit. Extremely athletic, highly trained, and skilled at all aspects of technical climbing, Simone craved being in the front, at the sharp end of the rope. Several weeks into the expedition, JC, Simone, and I planned to make a summit push together, as most of Simone's teammates had given up for one reason or another. We would make a very strong trio, helping each other with not only the physical tasks of breaking trail and carrying equipment, but also the psychological task of keeping each other motivated. Unfortunately, a few days into our summit push Simone, struggling with a health issue, started to falter and fall behind JC and me. In the end it was via a shouted conversation that Simone told us he was heading back down. Knowing that he would get weaker and be a liability going higher, he opted to descend while he could make it on his own, hoping to recover and make another attempt.

I was quite impressed with his prudence, yet sad that he would not reach the summit with us the following day. A week later he felt strong enough to make a solo attempt for the summit, but the storms of Nanga Parbat prevented him from succeeding.

Since that time, I have followed Simone's career with interest. In 2005, climbing with a Polish partner, Piotr Morawski, Simone at last stood atop Shishapangma as the first non-Pole to reach the summit of an 8000-meter peak in winter. A few years later, teamed with Denis Urubko, of Kazakhstani descent, Simone reached the summit of Makalu on February 9, 2009. Next he summited Gasherbrum II on February 2, 2011 with Urubko and the American Cory Richards.

Simone has shown that he has the patience and commitment to endure the hardships and, equally important, the wisdom to know when the game is up and it's time to retreat. He has made twelve attempts on Nanga Parbat, three in winter. I believe that turning back is not failure, if you've done your best. Simone has proven, time and time again, that he is willing to make multiple attempts before "succeeding." In the pages of this book, we get to experience some of his amazing journey with him.

As Simone said, "I will go in winter. Again. Yes, in winter. Just because it's my dream. Just because exploration never ends."

Ed Viesturs
Seattle, June 2014

PREFACE

I KEPT ESCAPING IT. I always had a thousand things to do, between family commitments, traveling, planning, going on expeditions, and training. Since all of these things demanded my work, attention, and energy, they became unassailable alibis for not sitting down at the keyboard to type. Yes, type, in an attempt to transform memories into words, re-creating the moments, months, weeks, and years spent living out my childhood dream in the vertical world. Forty-four alpine expeditions and forty-four years of life could have (and should have) resulted in as many books. I could have at least published some articles. But no. Since my first experience as an author in 2003, when Corbaccio published *Cometa sull'Annapurna* (*Comet Over Annapurna*), I've put off writing until the last minute, preferring action and storytelling over editors.

I just didn't want to sit down to write. For someone in his mental and physical prime, it is too sedentary an activity, an enforced pit stop. At the same time, I didn't want to delegate the task. I suppose I could have told a stream of stories to someone who would turn them into words on a page. But no, I never had anyone else do my essays for me in school. The same goes for my books, or climbing, or my path in life. And so I never began my second book, never "gave birth." I went on accumulating experiences, trips, and climbs but always postponed writing for some calm moment that I secretly believed would never come.

But this time I made myself do it, just like my daily training and household chores and responsibilities. "Now you will sit down and write!" Ten minutes or so of surfing the net and then I'd disconnect, managing to stop myself from escaping into the web. "Now you *will* sit and write, damn you! Ugh . . . what a pain."

Okay, but now what do I write? I won't have to tell everything from the start, will I? Retracing twenty years' worth of expeditions?!

Because my memory sucks. At best, I remember too little to fill the pages of a book. At the same time, though, I've never stood still, so I do know I have a lot to tell. What if I've forgotten many days, too many—facts and anecdotes that I'll never manage to string together from memory? No, I'll have to find another way to approach it. I have to find a theme, a central idea, something that will enthuse me, shed light on memory like a beacon, something to ease the hours I'll now have to spend here at the keyboard (damn it!).

I'll be leaving for Nanga Parbat in forty days and my agenda is crammed full of tasks. I suspect that only once there, in the surroundings I love best, will I find the concentration necessary for writing. When I said so to my editor, he probably thought I was insane. He said it would be almost impossible.

There! That's the key word, the theme of my book! "The impossible"—or rather, "the nearly impossible."

Becoming a full-time mountaineer was a nearly impossible dream. But as I said, I can't tell this dream from the beginning, at least not this time. So instead I'll share another "nearly impossible" thing about me—the thing that both lured and pushed me right from the start toward the coldest, highest, and most terribly beautiful mountain faces and summits of the planet. Yes, that's it. I'll tell you about winter mountaineering, about my winter ascents of the 8000-meter peaks.

Even if it turns out to be true that I can't fully remember my entire ultramarathon of vertical experiences from 1992 to today, it's very clear that winter is the subject and the season I'm most known for. Also, I love the idea of writing about this kind of mountaineering while I'm actually immersed in another winter expedition.

How beautiful! How crazy! I risk writing something already outdated, like a climbing guidebook or a road map or a book on the restaurants of Italy. The world I'll write about is constantly evolving and changing, just like me. In the end, what I'm setting out to do will be a snapshot of part of my life, with occasional close-ups of the most exciting and icy-cold moments when I felt extraordinarily alive.

Okay, we're off ... (ugh ... poor me ... !).

JANUARY 4, 2012
Nanga Parbat base camp (4230 m), -13°C

WE'RE FINALLY AT BASE CAMP. I sent some porters here at the end of October so they could make a rock shelter in which to set up our tent. We found it here today and it was very well made. These folks are truly wonderful.

Tomorrow, we go scouting. We plan to take a closer look at the wall and gain some altitude on the flanks of Ganalo Peak. But today was our first chance to relax. We stayed at base camp and set up a second tent. It'll serve as storage as well as dormitory for the two cooks and the sirdar (head Sherpa).

While we were working, a giant avalanche released from the high point of Mazeno Ridge. It's the longest ridge in the world and descends from the summit of Nanga Parbat toward the west. So we had the chance to see this force of nature close-up. The powder came all the way down to us, almost five minutes after the release. It seemed like it was snowing.

Of course, I haven't forgotten that my son, Jonas, turns two today. I Skyped him. We played and joked around.

CHAPTER 1

A TASTE OF WINTER MOUNTAINEERING

(CERRO MIRADOR AND ACONCAGUA)

MY LONG JOURNEY AND DEVELOPMENT as an alpinist, what they call a "career," started with winter mountaineering, right from my second expedition at age twenty-five. It was 1993. My attention had turned to one of the most difficult walls of the world, the south face of Aconcagua. At almost 7000 meters, Aconcagua is the highest peak in the Americas. In the shadow of this immense wall, in the middle of winter, Lorenzo Mazzoleni of Lecco and I had a splendid, magical, and nearly tragic alpine-style adventure. (There was supposed to be a third climber, but he didn't even start the climb.)

We were a couple of twenty-five-year-olds, completely self-sufficient, in total solitude on one of the world's most mammoth walls. We overcame all technical difficulties during the first 2000 meters of the climb. But then heavy snow ensnared us for several never-ending days at an altitude of more than 6000 meters. That white trap could have killed us. There was no way out under those conditions. We had almost zero visibility and very little gear on hand to face 2 kilometers of abyss. It became a dramatic and incredible race against death. We had to think up anything and everything in order to place the infinite number of anchors from which we suspended our lives and our hope during the seemingly endless rappels. In the end, we made it. We reached the base of the wall exhausted, like robots, incredulous and fazed by the dangers we'd faced. With hardly a word, we immediately put on our skis.

We knew we had another 40 kilometers to cover in extreme temperatures, without any energy reserves, in the dark. All night long, we broke trail toward the valley, trying to orient ourselves between one gust of wind and the next, knowing we'd be safe only if we managed to reach the road between Argentina and Chile where we'd started our adventure. We had no alternative, so there was no room for weakness or second guesses. Our only option was to never stop moving. Like hunted animals, we reached the hamlet of Puente del Inca at 2700 meters after two days of uninterrupted descent. Those twenty houses and a hotel seemed like the most beautiful, secure, and desirable place to be in the whole world. We were safe. We ate, drank, and rested for a few days, but we didn't want to go home without having achieved our goal. Besides, we still had the time and energy for another attempt.

At that time, no one organized expeditions on Aconcagua in winter, and it's rarely done even today. So we would be the first to make a second attempt. We knew we were well acclimatized after those long days on the wall. Also, before the south wall of Aconcagua, we'd climbed a new route on Cerro Mirador, a 6089-meter mountain adjacent to Aconcagua. We'd even slept on the summit. So, including the night we'd been stuck on the south wall, we'd logged almost a week at high altitude.

Knowing this motivated us to give it another try. We decided to take on the other side of the mountain by the normal route, conscious that, in winter, there wouldn't be anything normal about it. It would be a very demanding climb, lashed by wind and extreme temperatures. We aimed for speed and lightness. We put our trust in our proven teamwork and in our blood, rich by now with red blood cells. Once again on skis, we left Puente del Inca and soon arrived at Plaza Mulas, our base camp. This grind usually takes two days in the summer, with mules to carry supplies. We were the mules in this case, carrying heavy packs. We were welcomed to base camp by a beautiful sunset lighting the east side of the wall aflame, precisely the part we were to climb.

We left early the next day without bivouac supplies, equipped with the usual climbing gear. Our objective was to climb as quickly as possible, finding our way up the snow-clad slope of the mountain. The level of difficulty is notoriously modest, but in winter crampons are necessary. You have to be very careful not to get swept away by the gusts of wind that come suddenly and then go just as unexpectedly, giving way to an illusory calm.

In just thirteen hours, in the middle of winter, we reached the summit at 6962 meters, the highest point in the Americas. We stayed for about a quarter of an hour, maybe longer. We wanted to bask in the moment of our first significant winter ascent, accomplished completely independently. That might have been the precise instant I first glimpsed the joy and beauty of winter mountaineering. I got my first taste of the powerful, undeniable pleasure of this kind of climbing, a different approach that imbues a well-known mountain with renewed fascination and reveals new challenges, all through a simple change of season.

Climbing in winter, whether solo or in tandem, allows you to fully embrace the heights and view the panoramas with a gaze outside of time. You're free from the notions and opinions of any other mountaineers, free from their tracks, their noise, their stuff. You're aware of being, by choice, part of a world laid bare, a world where banalities have been stripped away along with the usual comforts, a world where sense and meaning are restored.

We descended immediately to base camp. All that evening and night, we savored the crystal clear, icy air that allowed us to see the glow of Santiago del Chile's lights nearly 200 kilometers away. The temperature dipped to −46 degrees Celsius that night, but no sensations of suffering surface in my memory. Of both climb and descent, I remember only beautiful things, pleasant things, like my friendship with Lorenzo, and the people we met when we were off-mountain during those two months in Argentina.

That was the second expedition of my life. I took home two winter ascents, of Cerro Mirador and Aconcagua, but above all I took home the awareness that I bloody loved the cold and the winter. Maybe I already knew, subconsciously, that this sort of climbing would be a constant draw, that I wanted to make it my life, my everyday routine . . . but I certainly never imagined that I'd one day write a book about my winter career!

On a winter expedition, you have to be decisive and extremely careful about every little thing in order to get back home, not only alive, but in one piece, without incurring serious frostbite and the subsequent amputations. We're talking about risks that are very real and well-known even in the most favorable of seasons. But in the case of winter ascents, the risks are higher, whether in the Alps or on Everest. So you have to obsessively follow unconditional rules of conduct and personally inspect everything. The timetable for summiting, the monitoring of speed, and the stages and procedures of climbing must never be delegated. Moreover, all decisions must be made strictly based on reason and not on emotion or impulse, which often cloud the mind with the desire to succeed, with ambition. If you want to win at all costs, death is often the result, or in the best case scenario, you survive by the skin of your teeth.

On a mountain, especially at higher elevations, you need to look within and listen to yourself, not compare yourself to others. There are no strong people or weak people at altitude, only people who are doing well or badly on any given day. I could give a long list of accidents on expeditions where rescue was called in from the high alpine, and others where people just got lucky. I'd say the percentages are terribly skewed toward the former.

But climbing can also be a nearly perfect kind of freedom. It's not just a sport. It's more than that. It's a kind of escape, a means of personal discovery, exploration, adventure, and contemplation. So it's only right, then, that each person should climb as he wishes, perhaps even making "mistakes" and apparently illogical decisions, as long as he doesn't drag others along or involve people who have altogether different intentions. I'm tired of answering to those who ask me to make judgments or rankings: there is no absolute truth, no "right" ethic, no "real" way to climb. I have mistakenly fallen into the trap of giving definitions, and I don't want to do that here. That's why I will tell the story of my winter mountaineering exactly as though it were my own face, my ID card. To each his own journey, and it's only right that I tell mine.

For me, talking about winter mountaineering is not about making judgments and expressing opinions about climbing in a certain way or in a certain season. Climbers have always been at each others' throats, often over bullshit, over invasion of territory. May the rigors of winter freeze this tendency in its tracks, at least in the mountains and in my words.

JANUARY 6–8, 2012
Scouting and acclimatization between Nanga
Parbat base camp (4230 m) and Camp 1 (5250 m)

WE'RE ALL SUPERMOTIVATED HERE. Wait times are, and
will be, long. I'm taking advantage of that to keep writing
my next book—to be honest, I should be submitting it just a
few days from now.

Today was also an opportunity to shave and get myself
together. Then, we started another day of going back and
forth from base camp to the Nanga Parbat face near Camp 1.

Numerous avalanches released during the trek. The
snow was inconsistent. Tiny slabs broke beneath our feet.
This seemed insignificant at first but revealed the fresh
mantle's instability. An avalanche to our right made us realize
we were taking unnecessary risks. So we left a supply cache
in a secure location and went back to base camp.

Today, we finally saw the sun again—hello there!—and it
hung around for a couple of solid hours. What a difference it
makes! I wish I could explain how important it is, especially
on a psychological level.

CHAPTER 2

IN ANATOLIJ'S NAME

(EVEREST AND MARBLE WALL)

AFTER THE POSITIVE AND EXCITING experience on Aconcagua in the winter of 1993, between expeditions I started spending more time on ice in the Alps. In addition to the sport-climbing season, I got into climbing waterfall ice in particular. This alternation of modes and techniques would prove very useful. My broad set of skills, and the resulting mental flexibility, would help me become an alpine guide and deal with many high-altitude situations.

Climbing really taught me how to expand. It permitted me to broaden my professional and cultural horizons. Going into the mountains gave me the chance to get to know a lot of people, build friendships, and even make some unique connections. The one with Anatolij Boukreev was definitely the most important connection I made, the deepest friendship I've experienced at altitude. I've shared a lot about him already, in articles, in my first book (*Comet Over Annapurna*), in talks I've given. I've answered the inevitable detailed questions. To avoid falling prey to singing his praises constantly, I'll limit myself to dedicating a few lines to him here, since my next winter experience following Aconcagua was in fact the tragic one on the south wall of Annapurna, roped in with Anatolij and Dimitri Sobolev.

I've recounted the climbing incident of that winter expedition elsewhere. I went home alone. Anatolij and Dimitri were gone forever. Their bodies, interred under thousands of cubic meters of snow and ice, were never found. Miraculously, that grave weighing many metric tons spared me. I survived an 800-meter fall in that same mass of snow and ice. It released at 6300 meters, from exactly the place where Anatolij was pointing a few days before, as I took his picture. I never lost my senses. I remember every instant. I knew that Anatolij and Dimitri were in the air, plummeting alongside me. I came to rest halfway down the wall, on the only ledge that could have stopped my fall, rather than mercilessly plunging another 1000 meters. It was as if a gigantic wave had swept us away. We were engulfed by it, pounded by it. Only I resurfaced, black-and-blue and bleeding. My hands and one leg were skinned and seriously injured. I found myself sitting, facing the valley, stripped almost bare by the force of the avalanche and buried in the snow up to my knees. Silence, only silence . . . then the cold and the shivering . . . I yelled my friends' names, again, again, and again. . . . Nothing.

That's how my first winter attempt on an 8000-meter peak finished— tragically. Hanging at 5500 meters, my thoughts turned to survival, to descending nearly one and a half kilometers while physically and mentally mangled. It was Christmas. No one knew our exact location. We had no way to contact anyone and we were isolated by a 2000- meter expanse of snow. What I faced in order to survive and get home was truly my most extreme adventure. Even today, I can't believe I managed to overcome all the internal and external challenges and single-handedly come up with a way out, a "self-rescue."

I got out of it alive but cursed to be alone, without Anatolij, my once-in-a-lifetime, irreplaceable friend. Much was at risk of remaining buried along with him: my enthusiasm, our plans, everything I'd worked for and dreamed about all my life, everything I'd believed was possible and was beginning to manifest.

I could have reacted very differently to such a violent blow. I could have given up on everything. I could have lost myself in memories and commemoration, feeding my remorse and making thousands of conjectures. Or instead I could react with awareness that even the most exciting things in life can never precisely match our desires, nor be exclusively happy and free of difficulty, as though untouched by reality. In life we win, we die, we love, we fight, we fail, we succumb, we begin again. Climbing is life, it's love, it's movement. So, naturally, it's subject to the unpredictable vagaries of existence.

After Annapurna, I simply had to go on so as not to die, so as to give meaning to my struggle and the dreams I'd worked toward and believed in.

And so I decided to continue going on the adventures offered by mountaineering. The vertical world wasn't the end of me. Instead, it was the means by which I was growing and discovering the world, searching out the most exciting and unknown part of life: myself. To abandon alpinism would have been to quit exploring myself, something I couldn't and shouldn't have to accept.

But my friendship with Anatolij had left me with not only a lot of unanswered questions and an ocean of curiosity to satisfy, but also a long list of alpine climbs I'd already set my mind to.

Above all, I wanted to get to know his country, his friends, Eastern European culture, the culture of the USSR, which no longer existed but was where Anatolij had been born and raised and come of age, as a man, an athlete, and later as a mountaineer. Traveling around the world, I had come across pieces of that crumbled communist reality: vehicles, and men who'd been assigned abroad and bribed to carry on with things that would no longer have been possible on ex-Soviet soil. In the mountainous regions, it was mostly helicopters and Russian pilots whose excellence I'd come to know. In fact, on that tragic winter expedition to Annapurna in 1997, I remember it was the excellent Russian pilot Sergey Danilov who took us to base camp at 4200 meters on board an Mi-17, that Spartan and all-powerful flying machine.

That might have been the very occasion on which I fell in love with helicopters and began to admire their versatility and usefulness. It may have been Sergey himself who planted the seed in me that later sprouted, leading me to become a pilot and to conduct rescues in the Himalaya almost thirteen years later. Once again, it was a Russian who gave me the basis for broadening my horizons and reaching for new loves and a new job, this time as a helicopter pilot, which has now become an increasingly significant part of my daily life. By a strange trick of fate, it would be Annapurna and another Russian pilot whose first name escapes me, a Captain Alexander, who would give me the final, friendly push in 2004.

I was going back to Annapurna to reattempt the summit with Denis Urubko. Like Anatolij, Denis was a Russian with Kazakhstani citizenship. We were just back from an exciting first ascent of Khali Himal (or Baruntse North), where we'd opened a new 2000-meter, alpine-style route with our third and unforgettable companion, Bruno "Camos" Tassi. Given the lateness of the season and since we were already acclimatized, we planned to fly to the base camp on the north face of Annapurna. I'd met Alexander the night before. After a dinner of fish, with quite a lot of wine (and vodka) on the table, he said, "You're doing the flying tomorrow. You know where to go better than I do, anyway!"

It struck me as the typical drunken parting shot to end the night, so I didn't take him seriously. But the next day, we had just taken off from the Nepalese airport at Pokhara near the lake when I heard Alexander call me: "So, what are you doing? Backing out?"

"No, no, if you let me, I'll try it for real."

"Of course I'll let you. I told you so last night!"

Alexander had the copilot get up and I took his place. I took the controls in hand and let myself be guided by a few brief instructions. Then Alexander said, "Perfect, that's good. I can see you're on the ball! Now take us to base camp and call me when we're nearly there!" He turned to the flight engineer and the copilot and they got talking.

Incredible! Only a Russian pilot would have entrusted me with a fully-loaded 7.5-metric-ton beast. True, he was still in the pilot's seat, ready to take things back in hand. But I felt a wave of responsibility that could have overwhelmed me in a nanosecond.

The flight was thrilling. I looked down on mountains I'd previously seen in photographs or when walking along the valley bottoms. Some I had admired from afar, from the summits of other big mountains I'd climbed. But flying alongside and through them was unforgettable. Everything went smoothly. After that flight, I knew that this would be my other passion. Doing something for the people of Nepal had already been on my mind for a while. The idea of creating a heli-rescue service immediately struck me as the most thrilling way to meet the country's most urgent need. I knew from personal experience how important the helicopter was. It had saved my life at the end of that fantastic descent following the 1997 avalanche, and it had also often helped me transport expedition loads when the porters weren't able to do it. What's more, helicopters had the potential to become an essential means for creating hydroelectric stations, transporting supplies of large size and weight, and quickly evacuating the ill, the elderly, and mountaineers.

In short, I have always gotten along with Russians, or Soviets, or whatever you want to call them. And to think that they're considered the "bad guys," if you go by what Western film and propaganda have given us to understand. So, yes, it's always better to discover the actual truth about things for ourselves rather than go by what we're told.

Certainly, you should never expect a lot of favors or courtesy from Russians, nor should you expect much mediation, politically correct expressions of opinion, or other "soft" gestures. But for someone of my disposition, and for high-altitude conditions, I think they're the best kind of people to surround yourself with, especially if your objective is a winter ascent or a particularly difficult climb. At least if they tell you where to go, they say it to your face and not behind your back.

Apart from wanting answers to the many questions left hanging with Anatolij's passing, this extraordinary rapport was precisely why I decided to go to the Pamir and Tien Shan a year and half after the 1997 tragedy. I wanted to make the "Snow Leopard project" happen in a single season, traveling through Kazakhstan, Kyrgyzstan, and Tajikistan. There are five 7000-meter peaks in the former USSR, then known as Pik Lenin, Pik Komunism, Pik Korjenevska, Pik Khan Tengri, and Pik Pobeda. During the Soviet era, those who climbed all of them in the span of their career were given the Snow Leopard award. What I wanted to make happen that summer of 1999 was the project Anatolij and I had come up with: completing this alpine marathon during a single expedition—albeit aware of the logistical and political difficulties presented by three independent, and not always peaceful, republics.

That crazy adventure, one of the most beautiful expeditions of my life, deserves an entire book. I renewed my promise to do it, but with four hands instead of two, with Denis Urubko. Denis in fact became the most exciting answer I found to my many questions during the 1999 expedition. A new and different Anatolij Boukreev, Denis has been like a brother as well as my partner for climbing, mountaineering, and expeditions ever since. I met him in those former Soviet mountains, through Anatolij's people. Ours wasn't a lightning-fast, instant friendship sparked at first sight. We sussed each other out over the nearly two months of the Snow Leopard project. We got to know and understand one another and eventually bonded with a strong feeling of friendship that remains unmatched to this day.

After the thrilling experience of '99, I felt completely like myself again. I had fully recovered from the '97 avalanche and the loss of my dearest friend. I felt happy again, positive, and I wanted to pick up where I'd left off: in winter, at high altitude, with a Kazakhstani climbing partner. I still had the burning desire to climb from a place of exploration rather than "peak bagging."

In 2000, I gave Denis his first invitation to come to Nepal and attempt Everest with me. Along with the invitation came another gift: his first Kazakhstani passport and the possibility of travel. It was a special expedition. We climbed the highest mountain on the planet together on May 24, after having spent four nights at 8000 meters without bottled oxygen. We were also short on food at our final camp, the South Col, which is the size of two soccer fields, swept by winds, suspended between Nepal and Tibet. Enduring those altitudes for such a long time without oxygen dramatically erodes the body and mind.

Staying up there without food or fuel is another huge risk. That's why we rummaged through the fuel canisters and food left behind by previous expeditions. I remember we found some cheese. I can still see the label and the writing on it: "New Zealand." Who knows how long it had been there. . . . I gobbled it down without sharing, and then Denis and I tried to drink some hot tea. Not many hours later, though, I wasn't well. My vomit was dark. Probably what was coming up was bile, but the dark color scared me. I was afraid I was vomiting blood. Denis was worried. He left the tent and managed to find an oxygen mask and a half-full cylinder from a commercial expedition.

I used the oxygen for a few hours. Then, the moment we'd planned to leave for the summit came, around midnight. The mask was plastic, not well-suited for high altitude in my opinion. After leaving the tent and setting out for the top, I felt less benefit from the supplemental oxygen as time went on. I thought it was due to my weakened condition, so I gritted my teeth and kept an eye on the number of steps I managed to take between breaks, and the length of the breaks, just as I had been doing from the start. I was trying to monitor my rate of ascent and my state of well-being based on these simple yet accurate signposts. I was willing to suffer through it, to take it step by step, but only if the thing was doable at a constant pace and speed. That way, I could reach the summit within the predetermined schedule, without any delays.

After the 8400-meter mark, I was slightly behind Denis yet keeping up an acceptable speed. But the weather was noticeably worsening. Visibility was getting more and more limited and the wind was getting stiffer. The situation was still manageable, though, and somehow I struck a balance between my shortness of breath and my progress. Still, something seemed off. Usually, when you slow down yet keep climbing, your strength diminishes conspicuously. You get less and less lucid. Your rest stops get longer. Yet nothing of the sort was happening to me. It was just the usual shortness of breath and those ten, inescapable, steady steps before the thirty-second pause, during which I tried to breathe as deeply as possible and regain my strength for the next ten.

I was expecting the cylinder to run out, since I'd already used it during the night and had been climbing for four hours by then. Below the south summit, at nearly 8700 meters, I finally understood the absurd explanation for this odd situation. The transparent tube connecting the bottle to the mask was blocked with ice, especially the part near my mouth. The oxygen, which likely had run out a good while before, was replaced by the moisture from my exhalations, which froze and plugged the tube. Basically, I was climbing with a mask that covered both my nose and mouth; and not only was that mask not feeding me oxygen, it was limiting my ability to breath the outside air. Once I realized this, I tried to break up the ice by bending the tube. Actually, the mask had some advantages. It protected my face from gusts of wind. And it humidified the air as I inhaled, which I breathed much more gladly than the cold, dry air around me. Every so often, I tried removing the mask and taking deep breaths, but then I'd put it back on so I could feel the warmth on my face again. I didn't have a cloth or neoprene mask to use instead.

The summit was very close by now. All of a sudden, Denis appeared. He'd started his descent after having been on top of Everest without oxygen. I still remember his astonished eyes and his shout: "Wow, Simone! You're here?! Well done, come on, go for it! The summit is just up there! I thought you'd turned back a few hours ago already. But here you are! What would you like me to do? I can wait for you here if you want and we'll go down together."

I took off my mask and smiled at him.

"Hey Denis, take it easy, I'm okay. . . . Shit, my mask is all iced up. I was having trouble breathing for hours and didn't get it. . . . Go ahead and head down. I'll go up, take a couple pictures and catch up with you. See you at the South Col tent. Just have some hot tea ready, that's all."

In only a handful of minutes, I was on the summit all alone. Then two ice-encrusted Sherpas showed up, without clients. It was foggy. You couldn't see more than a few meters but I wasn't worried, because of the fixed ropes from South Col, a sort of Ariadne's thread that showed the way down. Also, the ridge of Everest is very obvious, so it's impossible to get lost in those conditions. And besides, the wind had died down with the arrival of the clouds.

For both Denis and me, it was our first time on Everest. I would have preferred to get there in a different way, of course, but when all was said and done, we'd spent five nights at 8000 meters without oxygen, and I'd gained a fuller awareness of my abilities, something that would serve me very well in the coming years.

Also, Denis and I emerged from the Nepalese experience with an even stronger friendship. We'd understood our potential as a successful climbing partnership, a sincere and cheerful one. Mountaineering-wise, I'd been raised on the feats of the great climbing duos: Messner-Kammerlander, Kukuczka-Wielicki, Loretan-Troillet, all of whom I studied and admired. So when I got to know Anatolij, I thought I'd found a perfect partner. I was lost after his passing and skeptical about ever meeting another person like him, someone with whom I could establish so deep a connection.

Nevertheless, between the Tien Shan and Pamir in 1999, and Everest the following year, I'd set about finding a new, exceptional partner and . . . now realized I'd found him: the same nationality as Anatolij, the same athletic physique of a soldier, the same climbing heritage, but different in terms of character and age. "Spartan" and "powerful" are terms I've used to describe both Russian helicopters and the people of that country. These same terms perfectly describe Denis and Anatolij. They're also the qualities essential for winter mountaineering, especially at extreme altitudes, or when you dream of doing a kind of mountaineering that's off the usual climbing routes.

Having found a perfect new climbing partner prompted my decision, that year after the Everest expedition, to get back onto the path interrupted by the tragedy with Anatolij. The time had come to go back to exploratory winter mountaineering, once and for all. To do it in the best possible way, I would need to be not only with Denis but also close to Anatolij . . . so I decided, as with the Snow Leopard project, that the objective would again be a mountain close to Denis's home. I decided to attempt the first winter ascent of Marble Wall (6400 m), locally called Pik Mramornaya Stena, the most northerly 6000-meter peak of central Asia. The summit is on the border between China and Kazakhstan. It's in the vicinity of Khan Tengri, which at 7010 meters is the highest mountain of Anatolij's country. I had already climbed Khan

Tengri with Denis in forty-eight hours, round-trip. You can reach the Marble Wall base camp at 3400 meters with an off-road vehicle. After that, it's a 3000-meter incline and a long process of climbing to get to the summit. So the mountain's size and the altitude are significant. Plus, its very northerly location makes Marble Wall a glacial, arduous mountain, especially if attempted in the middle of winter.

But this attempt wouldn't include only Denis and me. It wasn't yet time for him to leave the group style of mountaineering, which I refer to as Soviet, not to be critical but to emphasize that the final outcome matters more than any given individual's personal abilities, vision, or ambition. At Marble Wall, in fact, we would be part of a large group of fifteen, all with the same climbing objective but taking two different paths. I would be the only Westerner, carrying the extra responsibility that came with being "Anatolij Boukreev's friend." I knew that the team would be observing me constantly, curious to understand what had convinced Anatolij to rope in with me for his final adventures a few years before.

I didn't leave Italy alone, though. I had a friend from Bergamo along. He'd been helping me look for potential sponsors for a few years. Decidedly not a mountaineer, Giovanni Ghidelli has always been a different sort of person, a likeable and blatantly out-of-the-ordinary character. An accountant by profession, he's always been inspired by the possibility of deepening his knowledge of the world, the one not found in guidebooks. A winter trip to Kazakhstan struck him as an opportunity not to be missed, so he asked if he could come along. His interest was probably not strictly educational. He's always been a lover of the fairer sex and was curious to see what Kazakhstani women were like, up close . . .

At that time, the capital of Kazakhstan was still Almaty, and 95 percent of the country's population was concentrated there. Today, Astana has taken a big slice of that pie, but Almaty remains much more beautiful and livable than the actual current capital, which sprang up from nothing in the middle of the desert. When I speak of Kazakhstan, even today people ask me where it is, or they imagine a tissue-sized patch of insignificant land in the middle of nowhere. Instead, we're talking about a country almost as large as Australia. Almost everything under the sun is found on Kazakhstani soil, so much so that the country is considered among the potentially richest of the future. Mountains, glaciers, water, desert, petroleum, natural gas, gold . . . all that the world seeks is found in Kazakhstan, a huge country inhabited by only sixteen million people (compared to the sixty million on our narrow Italian peninsula).

Mountaineering on all the continents gives me the opportunity to study and understand societal dynamics. In those first months of 2001, I was to experience a type of mountaineering I had only read or heard about. The expedition to Marble Wall, in fact, was decidedly military in character. There were clear hierarchies to follow and orders to execute without debate. The head of the team and the project was Rinat Khaibullin, a longtime friend of Anatolij's. They'd even had some significant Himalayan experiences together. Rinat was very strong. Back in the Soviet era, he'd been selected for some of the most demanding expeditions in mountaineering memory: from the traverse of the four summits of Kanchenjunga, to the new route on Dhaulagiri's west face, and beyond to the sensational first ascent of Lhotse's south face. Despite two nights spent near the summit above 8400 meters, he'd been the only one to return without frostbite. Rinat had in fact been the only one to understand that moving through the final stages of the summit bid, from 8400 to 8516 meters, would entail enormous risk and serious frostbite. He gave up the undertaking and instead immediately readied himself to provide first aid and rescue to the other two climbers who came back from the summit with devastating frostbite on their hands and feet, so severe it led to amputating almost all of their digits to the first knuckle.

After the Annapurna tragedy with Anatolij and Dimitri, Rinat had also been one of the few to join me in Nepal to look for the bodies of my two friends and climbing partners. Our bond was strengthened and affirmed by that undertaking. It was he who organized the Snow Leopard project for me in 1999 and prepared the six months of difficult selections to "deliver" my partners for that marathon of 7000-meter peaks in the ex-USSR (Denis Urubko, winner; Andrey Molotov, runner-up).

In 2001, it was Rinat, once again, who accepted my request to participate in the Marble Wall winter ascent. He formed two teams on two different itineraries but on the same mountain and with the same objective. Rinat would guide a team of six in their attempt to open a route to Karly Tau (5300 m) and traverse the ridge to the plateau below the summit of Marble Wall. Denis and I would instead follow the classic route with the others but alpine-style, as always.

I was definitely the least acclimatized because, living in Bergamo at 270 meters, I don't often have the chance to climb at altitude. Almaty is instead situated at 900 meters, with mountains that exceed 4000 meters forming a beautiful backdrop to the city. The mountaineers in my group were used to going up and down these mountains, especially before an expedition like the one we were about to do. One of the most often climbed was Pik Konsomol, a.k.a. Pik Nazarbaiev, after the president of Kazakhstan.

Meeting this expedition's group of climbers assembled on the parade grounds of the military barracks, I was immediately struck by their gear. From the diversity of models and ages, you could tell at a glance who'd been part of some past expedition, who'd been given his gear as a gift from some passing climber, and who had inherited theirs as hand-me-downs from generation to generation.

I was—almost shamefully—the most decked out, all put together and flashy. It wasn't a very promising start. I could tell they regarded me more with scorn than admiration. In short, I had yet another thing to prove—that beneath the expensive clothes and latest gear was a locomotive, not just a shiny red wagon they'd have to pull along. They were all pleasant, though. I sensed I had a get-out-of-jail-free card because of my Annapurna friend.

We didn't stay in Almaty long and set out immediately for Marble Wall. We had a truck with six tractor tires called a Ural, and a jeep. I knew the route. I'd already driven through a large part of it in 1999 to get to Khan Tengri. The season and the context were very different this time, though. I clearly remember the long gridlines in the desert zone, with the Khan Tengri pyramid rising some hundreds of vertical meters above us. The cold and the wind made for a clear sky, so these natural contrasts were even more surreal, magical. We traveled for kilometers in the nothingness, with a snowy chain of mountains far on our right horizon and a desert landscape with a few dunes on our left. Every so often, we came across a small village with busted-up cars, a few tractors, broken-down fences, and very few people around. I don't recall if these men in the emptiness wore peaceful or sad expressions. I recall only one or two little boys who observed us closely and then went back to playing with their handful of friends. I also remember some horses, standing motionless in the middle of nowhere, staring into space with their manes blowing in the wind. In those unreal surroundings and with muffled sound, moving ahead slowly in the intense cold, we were awakened now and again by the truck's wheels squarely hitting one of the many potholes along the road.

After some hours of travel, we got to a hilly region that gave way to mountains and alpine vegetation. The mountains, which not long before had seemed always and forever in the distance like some kind of backdrop, were finally getting closer. All of a sudden, an extremely long enclosure grabbed my attention. It was parallel to the road and a only a few meters deep. It wasn't the usual fence delineating the perimeter of private lands. No, that two-meter-tall wall topped in barbed wire had a military feel about it, something menacing. I'd passed this way two years before, but it had made so little impression on me then that I didn't remember it now. That long, very long, barrier ran along the road, always. Every so often, there was also a sentry box. Although empty, they got the point across: best not get tempted to climb over and see what was on the other side (even if that were possible).

"Denis, what is this thing? What's on the other side? A military zone?" I asked.

"No. That's China over there. Actually, it's a buffer zone. It isn't quite China, but still, better to give it a wide berth. Let's call it a sort of no-man's-land before the border of national territory itself. And soon you'll see the Kazakhstani military base of Accol, do you remember it?"

"Of course, I remember it well."

"Right. From there, we'll keep going to the miners' shacks."

"Miners?" I asked.

"Yes, you'll see. We go climbing in the winter because we like it and we want to. But there we'll find miners who spend the entire season in the cold."

The road got increasingly narrower and bumpier. At a certain point, a steady rise of about 50 meters appeared around the bend. It was totally covered in ice, exactly like a riverbed. To our right lay the cliff face against which the road had been dug; to our left, a precipitous slope. Best not to slip, not even on foot.

"Fuck, what do we do now?"

"No problem," said the driver. "We have shovels and there's dirt and sand all over the place. There's fifteen of us. We'll spread this crushed stone all over the ice within minutes and we'll drive over it, you'll see."

We did exactly that. After twenty minutes, the truck (with the craziest of us still aboard) pulled up onto the ice and slowly covered that stretch of road, with a couple of skids that didn't bode well. Somehow—and with the help of a legion of saints—the whole thing ended in a smiling display of the driver's gold teeth, once he was out of danger. He made a show of being confident but I think he'd shit himself a little.

We finally arrived at base camp, or rather, its cement-house equivalent, a kind of small barracks. It was near a stream and from there, a steep ascent with endless hairpin turns began switchbacking up the very long ridge of a mountain. After countless curves, the road abruptly ended and disappeared into the mountain. The gold miners Denis had described were actually there. They sank down into the mountain for kilometers.

We unloaded the gear and set up in one of the big, empty, freezing-cold rooms of the building. Like a true leader, Rinat took charge and laid out the plan. Two teams, two different climbing routes, and the same objective: the first alpine-style winter ascent of Marble Wall.

We left the next day, six of us in one direction and the nine others in the opposite direction. It wasn't an 8000-meter summit, but climbing alpine-style without acclimatization to 6400 meters in winter struck me as anything but ordinary. Actually, I was afraid it would be almost impossible. I wasn't the only one who felt that way. So our team decided a first installment to 5000 meters would be necessary. We'd then go back to base camp before leaving again to attempt the summit. Rinat's team, however, had already acclimatized over the previous weeks.

On the first day, we were to cross along the ice lengthwise for 10 kilometers and set up the first camp on Marble Wall at 3600 meters. The second day we would climb to 4300 meters, beneath a promontory of the Marble Wall known as Pik Uzlovaya. On the third and last day of acclimatization, we wanted to climb and traverse Uzlovaya to 4600 meters so we could then descend to the col that separates it from another, higher promontory called Pogranichnik Peak (5100 m). We'd climb that, position our final camp beside it, and spend the night. And lastly, we would go back to base camp at the barracks to rest before the actual summit bid.

We followed that schedule. From the start, Denis and I tried to stay in the lead, finding the route and the best way through the moraine. Maksut Jumayev was with us, with Andrey Barbashinov and the other climbers to follow.

Many years have passed, but I still remember that one of the climbers had essentially no real climbing gear. Some of his teeth were gold and others a gray metal. He wore a gray overcoat, velvet pants, leather boots, and crampons with straps. Regardless, he carried on happily and undeterred. Everyone maintained a regular pace. Only near the end of the glacier did it start to decrease, at the first couloirs, on top of the moraine that we had finally put behind us. There was little fresh snow on the glacier and the going was fairly easy. The night passed peacefully, without any headaches.

The following days unfolded exactly as planned. We climbed to Camp 1 and Camp 2. The group kept spreading out more and more due to the difficulty, the possibility of encountering crevasses, and the safety procedures to prevent potential slipping and sliding. For that reason, we traveled roped in threes. I was tied in with Denis and Maksut.

It was cold. We started to do up our jackets securely and use heavier gloves.

We passed the 4000-meter mark. Fatigue was setting in. Our packs were heavy, we'd trekked and climbed all day, but we were satisfied. By now we were ready to set up the first camp and longing to dive into our sleeping bags. We had gorgeous, 6000-meter mountains in front of us, some of them as yet unclimbed. The one that most captured my attention was Pik Kazakhstan, with its perfect pyramidal form and rounded summit—very similar to Pumori, the mountain that rises west of Everest.

Not all the climbers arrived at the first camp together that night. No one was racing to get there ahead of anyone else. Instead, each kept his own pace, taking advantage of the clear skies and good conditions on the ridge. Meanwhile, on the other route, on Karly Tau, Rinat Khaibullin and his team were carrying on.

The second day of the climb was much more complicated. By then we were dressed in the warmest clothes we had available: high-altitude suits, Himalayan climbing boots, mittens, and goggles. Wind gusts had become more intense, and cold crept in everywhere. The point we'd reached on the ridge was dangerously rich in cornices and snow meringues pitched toward the opposite slope, toward China. From this very exposed place, we could see far beyond, toward the Blue Empire, and the view was lunar: an infinity of white mountains and valleys, glaciers, cliffs as far as the eye could see. No sign of humanity, homes, roads. Nothing.

We advanced very cautiously along that ridge, one at a time, always roped in and with our partners ready to arrest any possible fall or cornice collapse. We often had to stop suddenly to seek shelter from the wind gusts. Our huge packs acted like sails, catching the wind and further ratcheting up the tension. We finally reached the summit of Pogranichnik Peak in the afternoon and then descended to the col joining it to Marble Wall. With mechanical, essential movements, we quickly put up the tent and dove inside. The wind was building in intensity and we wanted nothing more than to get out of it and warm up. Not being acclimatized drastically reduces the human body's ability to generate heat precisely because of the scarcity of oxygen, that fundamental element in the process of producing all of our energy.

Our companions arrived soon after and pitched their tents too. Illuminated by the glow of our headlamps, our tents stood out against the starry sky, three yellow dots suspended in the dusk between Kazakhstan and China. That thin nylon cloth held up by a few aluminum poles was our refuge. Those tents represented safety, comfort, coziness. Due to gaining 2000 meters of altitude in those first three days, we all had some degree of headache and some of us also had nausea.

During the night, the wind grew even more intense and we decided to go down as scheduled, bringing everything with us. In fact, we'd struck all of the camps we'd slept in. Since we were climbing alpine-style, we always moved the same tent. When the time came to go, we loaded everything onto our backs and started down toward the valley, leaving behind not a single meter of fixed rope.

The descent wasn't simple in the least. Our bodies had been weak-ened by prolonged exposure to the altitude, and the constant cold had left its mark.

In a single long march, we went back to base camp at 3200 meters, to the miners' "mini-barracks." A few miners were waiting and offered us a hot meal. I was hungry enough to eat anything, so hungry that I can't even tell you what was on the plate. I only know it was something hot, blessedly hot. Soaked with sweat, shivering from the contrast between what we were swallowing and the cold temperatures we'd suffered until only moments before, we jumped into our sleeping bags and fell asleep within seconds.

The night passed quickly and peacefully. No one wanted to get out of their sleeping bags the next morning. The warmth was like being in the company of someone you didn't want to part from. Each awoke on his own, without any prior planning. We wound up together over break-fast. We started to discuss what to do, when to set off for the summit. The conversation started out matter-of-factly. We talked about the mountain, about the cold we'd encounter, about the route. But then, as we got into the details and the plan of attack, I noticed the discussion was unfolding only between Denis, Maksut, and yours truly. That fact become more obvious as time passed and made it clear pretty quickly: it would be only we three who reattempted the climb. We also had to take into account that everybody, we three included, had removed all the gear and left nothing on the mountain, not even a cache. So it all had to be done again from scratch, and what's more, the wind had probably erased our tracks.

We left the next morning in the dark, with the cold at its most palpable. We divided the load equally between our three packs, taking turns leading. We reached what had been the ascent group's Camp 2 fairly quickly. Once again, we were going alpine-style. Our tracks had indeed been erased and we were starting from zero.

We slept well and climbed to 5000 meters the next day. We went beyond the most exposed part of the ridge and regained the highest point reached the week before. We quickly repeated the routine of pitching the tent and setting up our spaces inside. We ate and chatted until darkness enveloped our bright yellow dot on the col.

We left early the next morning as usual, but not before dawn. We needed to see where we were going, and the darkness would have stopped us from identifying the best route. We had a somewhat crazy idea in mind, especially given that it was winter. We wanted to attempt the summit from there, from 4000 meters below the summit, directly from our yellow dot.

We started maintaining a quick pace, trying to complete an extended rhythmic series of steps before we stopped to breathe. The cold was truly penetrating and we tried to stay warm by moving as much as possible. We kept up such a fast pace in the climbing and resting phase that I remember little of the morning, except that we reached 5800 meters, where we faced some rock pitches, some vertical and others easier.

And there, all of a sudden, the outlines of Rinat Khaibullin's team appeared. They had opened their new route across Karlitan, linked it with Marble Wall, summited, and slept on the rock band. Now they were coming down, tired but happy with their successful adventure. This charged us up, despite the increase in altitude hitting us. We were even more exposed to the winds, which picked up after we got past the rock band. The technical difficulty definitely seemed to diminish, but the physical and environmental challenges didn't. Instead, a true battle was beginning. We were unroped by then, each going at his own pace but each with the same idea in his head. Getting to the summit and descending directly to 5000 meters was our mission, but we wanted to manage the risk by checking on each other, making sure that the weather didn't get worse, and maintaining as constant a rhythm as possible. There was a steep couloir at 6200 meters that we went through one at a time in order to avoid sending rock and snow down on each others' heads.

Then, finally, having completed the final stretch of the couloir, there it was—the summit! A super sweet, uniform dome at the top of an easy, snowy incline. Denis was almost there, then came Maksut, and finally, me. The wind was threading its way in everywhere. Even though we were all zipped up, it seemed to get inside our clothes and steal our warmth. But we were happy to make those final steps. We had finally achieved the summit of Marble Wall in winter, in our own way, just the three of us. The top wasn't as beautiful as I'd imagined it, though. Due to the crazy wind, the summit was rocky, a kind of cobblestone surface nearly devoid of snow. I didn't like it. It gave the impression of a low summit, of an easy climb. On the contrary, we'd spit up our very souls and waded in snow up to our thighs to get there! One part of the summit was a little more sheltered, so there was a little snow. I decided to take my summit photo there. I wanted that moment to be beautiful all the way and pleasing to me, as I'd imagined it. A few photos, a quick video, and then immediately back down. We were tired, happy, and motivated to end the day right, back at our yellow dot. Visibility was worsening due to wind and blowing snow. We also wanted to get back quickly so we would be able to find our tracks, which would guide us easily out of the maze to safety.

Everything went well and by nightfall we were back at our 5000-meter camp. We shook hands warmly. The vibe was more formal between Denis and Maksut, almost military, but it seemed sincere. This describes well what their attitude toward each other was at that time and how their relationship would evolve. Together they would climb all fourteen of the 8000-meter peaks and would be part of the same military sports unit in Almaty. Denis was first to achieve the 8000-meter objective, in spite of some boycott attempts on the part of people theoretically close to him.

The next day, we reached base camp, where everyone was waiting for us, Rinat Khaibullin first among them. They welcomed us with hugs and thumped us on the back. They relieved us of our packs, gave us food and hot drinks. Then we started to talk, describing the climb and how it felt. We laughed and sang. It was a night of triumph, that night at the gold miners' shack, very peaceful and sincere. But our stamina had been rigorously tested and Rinat practically ordered us to bed so we could rest up for the return to Almaty the next day.

In the morning, we packed the bags to put on the truck. We took both a group photo and one of just the summiters. Then, all aboard, we were off to the Kazakhstani capital along the same road, dozing for a large part of the journey. The surroundings were unchanged, the same cold and desolation. We were a tired gang of happy men crossing a wild world. We arrived in Almaty, and Rinat and his team organized a party for the next day in a mountain dacha, inviting (surprise!) the women's alpine team he was head of. It was an amazing party. Rinat knew what he was doing, and his choices were spot-on from start to finish.

For me, that climb was the ultimate return to the point where everything had been dramatically interrupted on Annapurna. This time, however, the outcome was extraordinary. Answers to the many questions I'd wanted to ask Anatolij had been found . . . and I'd become a little bit Kazakhstani and Russian myself, as well. Also, Denis and I were devoted friends by then, and he'd definitively established himself as the right climbing brother and partner. Eastern climbers had proven to be the best choice for me, be that for my soul or my ambitions.

That winter ascent of Marble Wall had been a key expedition and a key success, and it formed the basis on which I rebuilt my desire to explore during the cold season. I had felt the presence of Anatolij's spirit strongly, accompanying me to the summit and all the way back down to safety. I understood that I'd done well not to stop dreaming and that I could, that I must, continue with mountaineering for adventure and exploration.

JANUARY 11, 2012
Nanga Parbat base camp (4230 m), -13°C

PARTLY SUNNY TODAY AND LAST rest day at base camp. Rest might not be the right word, given I've written all day. Doing it with frozen hands and a hot water bottle under the laptop is quite the stunt! Denis and I want to go to Camp 1 at 5100 meters, load up some of the gear, and keep climbing.

We met some Polish climbers at base camp. We just invited them to come visit us in our tent. It was a friendly and cheerful meeting, partly because we cranked up the stoves (maximum temperature reached 8 degrees Celsius). We hung out for a couple of hours chatting about this and that, not just about Nanga Parbat. There's not a trace of rivalry between us. They are definitely determined, but in a relaxed mood.

CHAPTER 3

A MERE STEP AWAY FROM THE DREAM

(SHISHAPANGMA, FIRST ATTEMPT)

NO ONE HAD MANAGED A winter ascent of an 8000-meter peak in fifteen years, since 1988. It was as though a curse had befallen the entire climbing community. The attempts were many and ongoing. Teams of various nationalities tried but no one succeeded.

The Polish had been first to come up with and act on the idea of climbing the giants of the planet during the most grim and severe of seasons. Because of the political and economic conditions of their country, they hadn't been part of the conquest of the various 8000-meter peaks in the 1950s and '60s. But in the decades afterward, they breathed life into a new sort of conquest, a new kind of vertical adventure at extreme altitude—a winter adventure. The "creator" and leader of the first amazing expeditions to undertake that incredible feat? Andrzej Zawada.

The first winter ascent on the planet, the highest and most famous, was of Everest. Krzysztof Wielicki and Leszek Cichy set foot on the summit on February 17, 1980. They used oxygen and decidedly Spartan gear, compared to what was available on the Western market. Then they did the south-southeast face of Manaslu in 1984, Dhaulagiri and Cho Oyu in 1985, Kangchenjunga in 1986, Annapurna in 1987, and to wrap things up, Lhotse in 1988, climbed solo by Wielicki. In this series of seven summits above 8000 meters, the names Wielicki and Kukuczka stand out, the stars of three of the first winter ascents.

All the summits were reached at the peak of winter, but some of these expeditions set out from Poland in November or the beginning of December. Today, the utmost clarity and honesty is required on this point. The dates defining the winter season have always been December 21 to March 21. In the Alps, no one ever dreamed of leaving for a winter ascent outside that period. In the case of the Himalaya, deviating from that norm was somewhat acceptable during the time of the pioneers, when it needed to be shown that these peaks could indeed be reached in winter. But these days, just as with the use of oxygen or the different styles and modes of climbing, the exact dates of both departure and summiting must be accurately communicated. Lovers of statistics even tend to differentiate between a winter summit and a winter expedition and summit, precisely to differentiate the expedition period from when the summit is reached.

But this is a technical digression, a very picky one, which takes nothing away from the fact that Polish climbers were the first to conceive of winter ascents and that such ascents have become their exclusive domain. How come? Why is it that attempts by other climbers in the same season failed, even those made by the most well-known mountaineers? There could be many reasons, but one is certain: those Polish climbers embodied the grit and perseverance of an entire people who forged character and willpower from the deprivation they were subjected to for centuries. No one surpassed their ability to endure inhumane conditions with scant means and modest equipment while clinging to a mountain face and to the dream of getting to the top. The difference lay in their minds and spirits more than in their muscles and technical abilities. But the generations change no matter where you are, and they don't always maintain the stamina and physical power of their predecessors. Fortunately, life's conveniences are more common now even in countries where they were once only a dream. It was this progress that thwarted the triumphant Polish charge toward the 8000-meter peaks in winter.

Perhaps the final blow to this unrepeatable generation of Polish climbers was the combined loss of two iconic climbers and role models, leaving a void that they are still struggling to fill: Jerzy Kukuczka on Lhotse in 1989 and Wanda Rutkiewicz on Kangchenjunga in 1992. In 2000, Andrzej Zawada also died. He was the "father" of the most important high-altitude winter expeditions, starting with the Noshaq (7492 m) in the Hindu Kush of Afghanistan in 1973. The loss of Zawada marked the end of an era, the last twenty years of which saw climbers from the Tatras increasingly playing a leading role, and not just on winter climbs.

Since that last successful 8000er by Wielicki on Lhotse in 1988, all attempts had been in vain. The Himalaya and the Karakoram repelled everything and everyone. No one had any luck. I was also on the list of those who failed, given my tragic winter expedition with Anatolij and Dimitri on Annapurna in 1997.

After my Marble Wall success, though, I'd regained my confidence, and my aptitude for winter mountaineering was confirmed. So, at the end of 2003, I decided to turn my attention to Shishapangma (8027 meters), one of the seven peaks yet to be summited in winter.

This smallest of the 8000-meter peaks became my new objective. Shishapangma means "the crest above the grassy plains," and locals call this Tibetan summit Gosainthan, Sanskrit for "place of the saint" or "abode of God." It's the only 8000er that lies completely within the territory of the People's Republic of China. Also, out of the fourteen giants on Earth, it's the last to have been climbed. The Chinese didn't issue climbing permits for it until they'd achieved the first ascent themselves. They did it with a squadron-like team, a large and inevitably successful one.

I wasn't the only one dreaming of a historic first on that particular mountain in the winter of 2003–4. As a matter of fact, I was part of an expedition that included six other climbers. Four were Polish (Piotr Morawksi, Darek Zaluski, Jacek Jawien, and the expedition leader, Jan Szulc) and two were Canadians.

The group was too big for my tastes, but the Polish presence motivated me and led me to accept a joining of forces. Our goal was the south face, the most difficult one but also the most sunny. There were two possible routes: the one named after Wielicki (who wanted to be with us and should have been) or Corredor Girona, the Spanish route that opened up a few hundred meters to the right.

Tibet is a stark and desolate place in the winter. Going there in that season is really not advisable. The road in from Nepal is always rough, flanked by damp rock faces and often covered in ice for long stretches. While Tibet in the summer is a wide-open plain that seems to stretch out forever, in the winter travel is more a crapshoot, burdening you with worries and problems before you even see the mountain. What's more, unlike in Nepal and Pakistan, porters don't exist in Tibet. Only nomads dwell on that 5000-meter plateau. And they have absolutely no desire to spend day after day transporting loads with their yaks in the cold of winter for the occasional expedition that ventures into the region. As a result, costs double or triple, as do the unknowns.

We were lucky enough throughout the first stage of the journey, though. And when we got to the base of the mountain, the conditions on the face seemed good. The strategy of climbing in groups on rotation proved to be effective as well. I recall managing to start climbing with 600 meters of rope attached to my harness, which I anchored with two pitons in the middle of the face. Actually, that day I'd decided to push my luck. The rope I was tied in to would be left in place to facilitate our ascent and descent. I set out quickly, with steady placements of ice axes and crampons. The pitch was fairly intense, around 55–60 degrees, but the ice was perfect. At a certain point, Piotr and Darek called out for me to stop. The 200-meter coil had run out.

"Start another 200 and I'll keep climbing, over!" I shouted into the radio.

"Okay, but isn't it too heavy? Can you keep going?"

"Yes, go ahead. Attach it so I can climb!"

We repeated that procedure twice. With the entire 600 meters deployed along the slope and still tied in to my harness, I struggled to hang on to my axes while placing an anchor to fix such a long length of rope.

We were very pleased and especially optimistic when we went down that day.

Trouble was on the way, though, and it wasn't in the form of weather or technical issues. Wielicki, who'd been forced to give up his place on the team for personal reasons, had agreed to include two Canadians in the group, with the obvious and understandable intent of distributing the cost among more people. One of the Canadians (I've forgotten their names) had already participated in a winter attempt on K2, while the other completely lacked experience. I don't want to be too opinionated, but I won't hide the evidence or my personal viewpoint, either. I think the two of them would have been more suited for a Sunday climb than an expedition of this type. Their training seemed truly inadequate to me, as did their physical strength. Also, their input on tactical decisions indicated limited experience and a lack of effectiveness.

For this reason, a rift developed within the group until we were, in practice, two separate expeditions. I climbed with Piotr. Following or alongside us were Darek and Jacek. We took turns leading very harmoniously. The Canadians climbed separately, but they weren't making much progress, mostly due to the weakness of the younger and less experienced of the two.

But while climbing, a much more serious and troubling problem than the two Canadians emerged. We couldn't find a place to set up our first camp on the face. We'd established advanced base camp on the glacial moraine at 5500 meters, then Camp 1 at the base of the face at around 6000 meters, and nothing after that. We kept climbing but couldn't find a place to pitch a tent, even our little one. With a tent pitched, we could have spent the night and set out again the next day from there. Nothing doing. Each time, we had to head back to Camp 1 and then go up again, always loaded down, never finding a level place on which to take a break and make tea.

Several weeks into the expedition, we were making good progress, but the final days were consumed by two problems: the Canadians and the impossibility of establishing Camp 2.

Piotr's and my shift arrived. Our turn to go back up the face. More coils of rope to carry up a pitch that gave no sign of letting up. Instead, it got steeper at times, forcing us to proceed more cautiously and slowly.

At one point, I shouted into the radio, "Piotr! I may have found a spot to dig a ledge!"

At these words, Piotr let out a shout too. It was already close to nightfall and we were getting ready to descend more than a thousand meters in the dark.

I immediately began tying my rope to two pitons for a nice anchor.

"Climb on, Piotr, the rope is anchored! I'll start digging while you come up, so we don't waste any time."

"OK, Simone, good job, I'll come up as fast as I can and give you a hand."

I didn't even respond. I hung my terribly heavy pack from the fixed-rope anchor and got on with shoveling. I hit ice almost right away.

"Sonofabitch! Ice here, too."

I moved over a little and found some fresh snow, but soon enough I hit ice again. I used my ax to break up the ice and widen the ledge. There was barely room to sit down let alone set up even a small tent. I kept hacking away with the pick, in a frenzy, almost angrily. I had to do it quickly. The sun had already set and the temperature was plummeting.

Piotr joined me. He clipped his pack to the anchor and immediately started hacking away himself while I took a breather. We had to spell each other because the fatigue, altitude, and cold were setting in. The ice was hard as rock but, laboriously, the ledge began to take shape and get wider. Then we hit rock.

"Fuck!"

"Come on, Piotr, let's dig a bit to the left here and maybe we'll be able to put up the tent anyway."

We scraped away, right to the last centimeter of ice, and then put everything up. It was a hanging bivy, with two-thirds of the tent resting on the excavated surface and a third hanging over the void. Once inside, we kept our harnesses on and anchored ourselves to the mountain. We communicated our "success" on the radio and a wave of optimism broke over the group.

We slept well, with no headaches or nightmares. The sun's arrival the next morning seemed the most beautiful gift in the world. After breakfast we got ready to climb and position all the rope that was left, a little less than 200 meters.

"I'll go today, you went yesterday," said Piotr. "Stay here and belay me. It won't take much to fix these last 200. It doesn't look that hard. If only I can make it to those rocks! Then I can set up a good anchor."

Everything went smoothly. Piotr managed to position the piton exactly where he'd hoped. He tied the rope to it and came back down to me. We drank some tea and descended directly to advanced base camp.

We were really happy. That camp at 7100 meters could yet prove to be an important step in successfully climbing the face.

We started to make optimistic plans at base camp, speculating on strategies to improve upon the failures that had held back winter mountaineering for sixteen years. Darek and Jacek rightly decided they would go sleep in the bivy too, to better acclimatize and so they could try to climb a little higher. We were almost at the end of our fixed ropes. That meant lead climbing the rest of the route, or simul-climbing.

And so it went. Thanks to the weather, which stayed "human" for the most part, the two Polish partners climbed to the bivy, slept over, and fixed another 150 meters of rope starting where Piotr had left off. Everything seemed set for a serious summit attempt. Or so we thought.

Now it was our turn. Piotr and I were determined, prepared, focused. We still had 800 meters to overcome, from 7250 to the 8027-meter summit, including climbing and descending the last part of the final south-face couloir without fixed ropes, not to mention covering the entire remaining ridge in a hurry as we became ever more exposed to the wind. But it was still doable.

Our night at 7100 meters was perfect. We were calm and managed not to think about what lay ahead. We were optimistic. We had the proper motivation and our legs were still strong.

We left at first light. We couldn't risk finding ourselves without visibility at the most delicate stage of the climb. Also, the sun would warm us up after the scarily cold nighttime temperatures. At forty below zero, we had to seal ourselves inside our mummy bags, heads included, so we could breathe the warm interior air. Oxygen was in short supply as it was, though, so every few minutes we were forced to poke our heads out for some deep breaths.

That morning, we quickly arrived at the highest point Darek and Jacek had reached. There, the couloir narrowed like an intestine and at certain stretches offered no more than 50 centimeters of ice to kick our crampons into. We were going up slowly, doing stretches of mixed climbing, securing ourselves with a dynamic rope we'd brought from base camp for the purpose. Hours were passing and the couloir seemed to go on forever.

We'd probably overestimated measurements of our progress, the camp, and the fixed ropes by about a hundred meters.

We kept our talking on the portable radio to a minimum.

"Man, this couloir is never ending, Piotr!"

"As soon as you find a spot to rest, stop so we can swap."

I did as he suggested, taking him in quickly. He was the one to head into the ever-narrowing bowels of that icy couloir. The rope was going up in fits and starts, a sign that the level of difficulty was compelling him to take breaks. But he was making progress regardless and I really hoped that each pull on the rope would be the last. Time was passing relentlessly and it was well past noon.

After about half an hour, I heard Piotr's voice on the radio.

"Simone, come up! I'm finally out of the couloir, in the sun, on the ridge. It's gorgeous up here!"

"Okay, I'm on my way!"

I climbed as fast as possible, cleaning some protection Piotr had placed. The end of the couloir came into view along with my partner's face looking in my direction.

I was wearing a neoprene mask, but the cold was so intense I could still feel it on my nose and cheeks. The difference between the external temperature and my warm, exhaled air had created a layer of ice on the mask.

I broke with the usual rhythm and covered the final meters without a pause. Joyously, I took my first step onto the other side. We were out of the Spanish route, now the first to take that route in winter. But our primary objective was to summit Shishapangma.

We were happy yet well aware of having 500 meters or so still ahead of us, and it was bloody late. We immediately began the march toward the summit, skirting some seracs and avoiding some crevasses. We were advancing as quickly as possible, but in addition to the fatigue, the wind and the cold weren't cutting us any slack.

Having arrived at an altitude of 7750 meters, we could already see the summit 270 meters above us. But it was 3:30 . . . late, very late.

"Shit, it can't end like this!"

Piotr looked at me without saying a word.

"It's three thirty, Piotr . . . It'll be dark in an hour and a half . . . "

"What are we going to do?"

I didn't speak for a few seconds, during which time I turned again to look at the summit.

"I'd really like to get up there, now that we've done all of this," Piotr murmured.

"But we have to go back, right away . . . we have the whole couloir to descend and we'll have to do it in the dark as it is."

"You're right. Shake my hand. We've done an amazing job!"

We hugged, patted each other on the back, looked each other in the eye, and started down together.

It was a long and tiring descent. We'd spent most of our physical energy during that long day and now we had to push ourselves in order to arrive at the tent with a little time to spare. It was still light when we got to the end of the couloir. We managed to downclimb to the last anchor just in time. By then, it was truly dark, but we had the fixed ropes and we continued our descent by the light of our headlamps. We were thirsty, cold, hungry, and we couldn't wait to get into our "luxurious" tent-swing. It's amazing how your perspective can change depending on the situation. A few days before, the tent had seemed like the most uncomfortable bivy ever, but that night it was a five-star hotel.

We managed to reach it safe and sound and satisfied. First things first. We melted ice for drinking water and hot liquids. Rather than being discouraged or disappointed, we were delighted. We were alive, and we'd done everything possible to reach the summit. But above all, we now knew we weren't dreaming the impossible. The winter ascent of an 8000er was indeed within our reach.

The next day, we went directly to base camp where we met up with the whole team. They congratulated and hugged us, and that very night while we were having supper together in the mess tent, Piotr and I started thinking about the coming days, about a second attempt.

The weather decided against giving us another chance right away, however. In fact, the weather progressively worsened as the date of the yaks' arrival approached. We devoted our last two days to packing everything and readying our bags. The wind was awful, so bad it prevented us from sleeping. It rattled our tents and lashed Shishapangma all night long.

As we started the trek down to the Tibetan town of Nyalam, two days' walk away, we all turned to look at "our" mountain. Certain we would finish what we had brilliantly started that winter of 2003–4, we bid Shishapangma not good-bye but "see you next time."

JANUARY 12–13, 2012

Scouting and acclimatization between Nanga Parbat base camp (4230 m) and Camp 1 (5250 m)

TODAY WAS A GOOD DAY because we reached the place where we'd dropped our cache in less than two hours. We picked everything up and kept climbing, got past the glacier in the valley between Ganalo Peak and Nanga Parbat. On the other side of the labyrinth of seracs and crevasses, we found the right route and went full throttle on the left flank of the moraine. In front of us is the Kinshofer, the route Lafaille and I opened together in 2003. Our position gives us the perfect vantage point for checking out the face.

We just got back into base camp. We slept at –30 degrees. It's unusual to witness Denis shivering with the cold. We've already decided not to do the Kinshofer. Instead, we'll try another, probably the one Messner tried in 2000. We've gotten to a spot at 5300–400 meters that gives us a spectacular view of Nanga.

CHAPTER 4

ON THE SUMMIT AT LAST

(SHISHAPANGMA, SECOND ATTEMPT)

I KNEW I'D SEE SHISHAPANGMA AGAIN before long. I also knew I wasn't the only one who wanted to go back.

Exactly one year after our first winter attempt, we were below the south face once again. And once again, in keeping with the iron-clad international standard of the start of winter as defined by astronomy, we'd started after December 21. This time the two Canadians weren't with us, only the Polish climbers. So the team was made up of four mountaineers (Piotr, Darek, Jacek, and me) plus an expedition leader, also Polish, who would coordinate and track everything from base camp.

At the end of November, a Nepali friend who worked for Asian Trekking had informed me in confidence that another mountaineer also wanted to attempt Shishapangma in winter. It was Jean-Christophe Lafaille, who had left France in November.

As soon as I learned of this, I calmly looked at the calendar and said to myself, "Well, it's autumn. Why would I run to Tibet and get into a race? First, it's not my style. Second, it's not winter. In fact, winter's another month away." I gave my Polish partners the news anyway, and they came to the same rational conclusion.

I've never been one to change the rules to suit myself, whether they apply to ethics, sports, or society. So, if winter starts December 21, I refuse to arrive in base camp before that date. And it's not just a question of numbers. Up until the first two weeks of December, weather conditions are perfect, in fact. So the procedures—the approach, the base camp setup, the rigging of the wall, and so on—all of them take place under optimal conditions. After that, everything gets complicated, almost hellish: snow that slows everything down, intense cold that freezes the hands and feet, wind that makes the base camp setup an adventure unto itself. So, this matter of December 21 is not a case of neurotic perfectionism. Rather, it's an actual fact that must be respected and accepted.

Things went the way you'd expect. Jean-Christophe reached the summit of Shishapangma on December 11, 2004, accomplishing an amazing solo climb and opening an alternate route between the Wielicki and the British routes. But it wasn't winter, and some of the photos posted online—picturing him halfway up the wall in nothing but a zip-neck sweater—in essence confirmed this assessment. By coincidence, I myself was in Nepal that same day, acclimatizing in the Everest valley. I was actually on the summit of Island Peak with some Polish friends. We, too, were only wearing sweaters.

I therefore considered it only right to clarify this detail, not to take anything away from Jean-Christophe. On the contrary, I had climbed with him and opened a new route on Nanga Parbat. A nice friendship was even forming between us. My "seasonal" objection to his climb—even though I expressed it along with my congratulations—set off a long-distance debate (possibly fomented by others) that incurred the animosity and criticism of a group of mountaineers, albeit a small one. But I was just leaving for Shishapangma, so I didn't pay attention to those attacks and instead decided to give it time. I was sure that the international alpine community would uphold the historical definition of December 21 as the start of winter.

Once in Nepal, in early December, our team headed into the Everest valley for an acclimatizing trek. The conditions were perfect, with clear skies and pleasant daytime highs. The temperature dropped at night, of course, but was still manageable. The porters carried on with their usual work, carrying food, perishables, and other urgent items to the villages located in the valley's upper reaches. There wasn't any snow yet, and the area's inhabitants were using the opportunity to stock up. We reached Everest base camp. On the way back we climbed to about 5800 meters, above the Pyramid—the international observatory established by Italians near Lobuche at an altitude of 5050 meters.

We followed the same route back down as far as Lukla. From there, we flew to Kathmandu on a Twin Otter. It was our last chance to have a shower, as well as prepare all of our climbing gear and organize the trip in to the Tibetan village of Nyalam by minibus and truck. We started our approach to Shishapangma from there, coinciding with the start of astronomical winter.

We'd calculated at least two months' worth of provisions and fuel. To move all of our supplies, we hired a caravan of yaks. We'd haggled for them via the government official we'd been saddled with, as per the law, by the Chinese authorities by way of the Tibetan Mountain Association. The transaction wasn't the easiest. Our supplies were overweight so we needed more yaks. The official was the same person I'd met on Everest in 2002. Not that he gave us anything for free, mind you, but he was rather kind and gave us the yaks at a pretty good rate—from which the Chinese skim an incredible profit.

The day after our arrival in Nyalam we climbed the nearby hill to acclimatize a little, then spent the evening chatting and socializing with the government official. The next day, a wreck of a Chinese truck came to our hotel to take us to where the yaks were waiting. It took about fifteen minutes to get there. The herd was made up of animals that belonged to seven or eight different people. Naturally, each of these people wanted to be the one to carry our loads and things got heated right away. After a bit, the following scene lay before us: all of our stuff still on the ground while we watched the owners pushing and shoving and coming to blows.

"They always do this when work is scarce and they want to get it at all costs. You have to watch out. Sometimes they pull knives," the government official told us.

So much for the peaceful Tibetan nomad stereotype. . . . The world is the same wherever you go—although Tibet remains a somewhat unreal, unique place.

At last, the loads were distributed equitably in proportion to the number of punches landed and thrown, and everyone seemed satisfied. The trek with the yak caravan lasted two days, during which the "yak drivers" (we would probably call them herders) more than once had to chase after and calm the animals, who wanted none of it and were bucking like horses. Yaks are exceptional, gentle animals but they're really scary when they get worked up.

We got to base camp near a lake that was clearly frozen. It would be our only source of water, as our Nepali cook, Jagat Limbu, well knew. The cook's Nepali assistant, Chhiring, was also with us. He'd been my cook the previous year during my expedition to Khali Himal. My memorable companion Jagat, on the other hand, is a jack-of-all-trades: cook, logistics whiz, mountaineer, and entertainer.

We set up our base camp on the south side of the lake. We each had our own little tent, in addition to the kitchen and mess tents. The latter was a recent model supplied by The North Face specifically for this purpose. It accommodated the whole team and provided some shelter from the polar temperatures we faced.

Jagat and Chhiring immediately went out to the center of the lake to make a hole and draw water, but the ice was so thick they couldn't manage it. They melted some pieces of ice they'd broken off with the pickax and told us they would try again the next day around noon, to see if the sun caused some water to gush out. Fortunately, their guess thereafter proved correct, at least on nice days.

The face was fairly free of snow, and the powerful wind seemed our only constant companion on Shishapangma. At times it was so strong up on the ridge that we could hear its rumble in base camp, a constant noise, loud and forceful.

The weather conditions in the days following our arrival at base camp allowed us to establish the advanced base camp, in the same place as the previous year. We didn't want to do the Spanish route again this time, though, nor the longer but less complicated Yugoslavian one. Mining our experience of the previous year, we had it clearly in mind to position a camp on the final ridge at 7400 meters, so we wouldn't find ourselves once again weighing the late hour against the impossibility of bivying.

Again, it was just the four of us doing all the work—no Sherpas and no oxygen. But thanks to the acclimatization we'd done in Nepal in the preceding weeks, we felt faster than we'd been the previous year.

Once advanced base camp was established, we positioned Camp 1 at 6500 meters, on a level area half the size of a tennis court and sheltered by a stable serac. We had fixed ropes up to that point. In the coming days, the ropes would speed up the repeated ascents and descents that were part of the process of the overall climb.

Terrible weather left us stuck at base camp for a few days. The wind was doing all it could to rip our tents away. We kept reinforcing them and anchoring them with additional rope. Finally, the sky turned blue. The cold was arctic but the winds moderate.

It was time for Darek's and Jacek's shift. They loaded a few hundred meters of fixed rope along with some food and fuel and left first for advanced base camp before proceeding to Camp 1 well up on the face. We kept in constant radio contact, and once we knew they were at Camp 1 we brightened up. That load of gear was crucial. The next day they would climb and fix as much rope as possible, possibly reaching an altitude of nearly 7000 meters.

Darek and Jacek were amazing. Despite the weather being truly awful the next day, they still managed to complete the task they'd set for themselves and returned to Camp 1 to sleep. They were tired but knew they'd done an incredible job. The wind had pounded them all day long—when they talked on the radio, you could hear that a crust of ice had formed over their mouths. When they got to base camp the next day, we welcomed them warmly and thanked them very much for their work. The weather remained terrible, though. It was icy cold and windy for the next few days, and Jagat was forced to melt chunks of lake ice because there was no liquid water.

I have a mantra: "It can only get better." I repeat it to myself ad infinitum when I'm on expeditions, and this was no exception.

And that's how things were, after only five days of bad weather and an unavoidable layover at base camp.

It was Piotr's and my turn to get back up on the face. Our plan was to carry more rope and try to climb as far as the ridge. In addition to the rope, we wanted to bring the tent, sleeping mats and bags, and the stove, in hopes of establishing camp at 7400 meters before going back down. We knew it would be very hard going, but we wanted to give it a try.

We tackled the usual winding journey to advanced base camp and then the climb to Camp 1 as before. The cold was asserting itself. The wind was strong but didn't impede our progress. We spent the night at 6500 meters, at ease and chatting a bit more than usual. When we talked with base camp, they told us the weather conditions would be the same, only much windier.

The forecasts were spot-on. The situation was tough but bearable. With overflowing backpacks, we got an early start in the hopes of catching the first rays of sunlight. We ascended the ropes Darek and Jacek had fixed. The ropes were well done and went to nearly 7000 meters. Now, it was our turn.

We took our packs off and pulled out the ropes that we intended to fix. We decided to lead alternately, and I went first. The terrain was mixed and a little more complicated than I'd expected. Nothing extreme, though. I was able to do 100 meters in a single pitch, equivalent to the length of one of the coils. Piotr went up the rope I had just fixed and kept on. Same distance, same dynamics. Then I moved onto what had become exclusively rocky terrain. So rock climbing was called for, but I did it with crampons on and ice axes in hand or clipped to the harness, depending on the difficulty. The pitch was vertical and very exposed. The wind gusts struck harder than ever and unpredictably. The closer we got to the ridge, the less shelter we had. We were at the mercy of the cold, and the wind made it even more biting.

Once again, it was Piotr's turn, and I decided to film him climbing the last tricky sections of rock. Even a 5.6 is demanding when you're wearing heavy boots, crampons, and bulky clothing and carrying bulging packs while breathing thin air. Piotr was fast and efficient and disappeared from the viewfinder of my video camera in a flash.

A sudden shout made me spring instinctively into position to arrest a possible fall . . . but it was a cry of joy.

"Simone, come up! We're finally on the riiiiidge!"

I climbed up as quickly as possible, partly because it was afternoon already so we had to hurry along. My lungs filled with the icy air but I kept "running" toward Piotr. I went along the rope that he'd just fixed and then along the final 50 meters of an easy couloir without fixed ropes. When I got to within a few meters of him, the wind whipped up a mini-tornado of snow and hit me in the face with it. What a welcome to the ridge!

Piotr and I shook hands, clumsily because of the mittens we were wearing.

"We have to put up the tent and get in, fast!" I told Piotr.

"Yes, yes, I've already taken it out of my pack. It's right here, ready to go."

We worked quickly, and soon the tent was open. Piotr got inside to keep it from flying off and I tossed in my ice-encrusted pack. To better secure the shelter, I used a few bamboo sticks that we'd brought along to serve as route markers. I looked for every possible way to anchor the tent more firmly. Piotr had spread the sleeping pads out inside and was melting snow. I had him pass me the tent's stuff sack, and I filled it with crusty snow to put aside for melting that evening and the next morning.

The objective had been met. We'd reached the ridge and set up the tent at the final camp. We'd also equipped the last part of the face, so we could now go to sleep satisfied and think of the next day's descent.

But something happened that night. Neither of us were able to sleep. It seems that without a word to each other, while listening to the tent fabric snapping in the wind, both of us were hatching a plan different from our original one.

At a certain point, in the dead of night, I sat up and freed a hand from my sleeping bag. I reached out, grabbed the pull tab on the tent zipper, and slid it open just enough to see outside. The sky was clear and the wind was stable. Intense, but not prohibitive.

"Piotr, you sleeping?"

"No, what is it?"

"There's a starry sky and the wind is strong but doesn't seem to be getting worse . . . What if we try for the summit tomorrow? What do you think?"

"I was thinking that myself," Piotr answered. "I wasn't sleeping, partly because I had that idea buzzing around in my head."

He sat up too. He turned on his headlamp and within seconds we found ourselves discussing the details.

"Okay, so here's what we do," I said. "Tomorrow we leave about six, empty, no packs, as light as possible. We're not totally acclimatized yet so we have to do our best to be fast. The turnaround time has to be final, as always. If both of us aren't on the summit by then, we go down. We have to get back here before dark. We don't have fixed ropes, just a few flags."

"Okay, let's do it. We'll bring our cameras and the video recorder. Nothing else."

The plan was set, and with that we lay down again, set the alarms on our altimeters, and fell asleep.

The next morning, we woke without our alarms. We got up at six, made a quick breakfast, and got going. We climbed with measured strides at a steady pace, followed by a pause to rest. We were gasping for oxygen. Then off again for thirty steps and another pause. And so on, steadily, taking turns breaking trail.

We were the same team, on the same ridge, during the same time frame as the year before. But this time we were fresher and setting out from closer to the summit.

Our oxygen debt increased as we climbed. We were breathing through wide-open mouths and the frigid air punched into our lungs. But we didn't have a choice. We had to climb fast and that meant subjecting our bodies to maximum stress.

Hours passed and we were getting ever closer to what seemed like the summit. At one point, we were forced to descend about 10 meters in order to get past the serac where we'd camped the previous year.

We stopped and exchanged a glance.

"Here he is, our friend from last year," said Piotr.

"Uh huh . . . " I said nothing more. The game wasn't over yet.

We kept climbing, more and more slowly. Every fifteen or twenty paces we stopped, hunched over our ice axes. But the sight of a rounded hump not far above us was spurring us on: it had to be the summit. Another four or five series of steps and we were almost there. Then it dawned on us that the ridge was still rising upward . . .

Without getting discouraged, we reached the hump and looked up.

"We're almost there, anyway," I said to Piotr. I had climbed Shishapangma's Central Peak in 1996 and remembered the higher reaches of the mountain clearly. From our position, we had a perfect view.

It was just past noon, so we were right on schedule for safety. The wind had become very strong and was now blowing in gusts, but we almost hadn't noticed it. We'd simply synchronized our march with the gusts. When they arrived, we'd stop and breathe. When they abated, we'd resume taking our grouping of steps.

We caught sight of the spindrift typical of windswept summits. Even though a minor change in slope obstructed our view of the summit itself, we could sense it, thanks to that lashing wind.

We took the last series of steps with heads bowed, not looking up. We wanted to relish the sight hitting us all at once.

Of that magical moment, I remember exactly this: Piotr and I were very close together, as though we were waiting for one other. The final six steps. Slow, savored, and immortalized in our memory.

And finally . . . the summit!

Hugs, pats on the back, then arms around each other, squeezing again. It was a moment of indescribable intensity, maybe because I had been looking forward to that summit since Christmas of 1997, maybe also because the stifled emotions of the previous year finally exploded. In that moment, Anatolij was with me. While I was looking toward Nepal, with wind and blowing snow in my face, I thought of him.

We photographed and filmed each other. The few words Piotr spoke up there, captured by the video camera, were clear and definitive: "This is the first ascent of Shishapangma in astronomical winter. It's very cold and the wind is insane."

On that day, January 14, at 1:15 p.m., wind gusts recorded at the same altitude as the summit reached a velocity of 32 meters per second, that is, more than 115 kilometers per hour (according to a triangulation of data collected by aerostatic balloons). The temperature was –52 degrees Celsius.

We stayed up there for a quarter of an hour. We also tried to radio base camp but the signal was likely too weak. It was just past one, so we'd have four hours for the descent. We headed down, much faster this time, following in the tracks of our ascent. It all seemed especially easy that day and we practically ran down the mountain. We were thirsty. Our throats were dry from open-mouthed breathing and not having drunk much at all.

We reached our tent at 7400 meters, happy. We crawled inside and started melting snow and making something to eat. At a certain point, Darek's voice came over the walkie-talkie.

Piotr answered, telling him we were in the tent. Nothing more.

"How did it go today? What did you do?" asked Darek.

"All good today, we went to the summit."

"And this is how you tell us?! You're awesome, congratulations, that's great! Terrific, terrific!" shouted Darek.

He and Jacek and the expedition leader, Jan, had arrived at advanced base camp, and then Jacek and Darek had continued on to Camp 1. When Jan and Jacek heard the news, they congratulated one another over the radio, too, and said they'd meet up with us the next day. Darek and Jacek would go on to 7400 meters and then make their own attempt on the summit the following day.

The night passed peacefully. The cold seemed to have eased off, a symptom of clouds gathering, and thus a sign of an approaching weather front. The next day was overcast and we started the long 2000-meter descent to advanced base camp. We came across Darek and Jacek at around 6700 meters. We hugged and I told them I was really happy for all of us. Then we said goodbye and continued down.

The weather was quickly deteriorating, with sleet in addition to cloud cover setting in. The worsening situation affected us only slightly, but it was worrisome for Darek and Jacek, who were climbing and exposed at very high altitude.

At 6300 meters I ran into Jan, who'd come up specially to give us a hug. He was moved. He'd devised and organized this expedition despite skepticism from a part of the Polish mountaineering community. And now he could leave feeling proud, both of his team and of the first non-Polish person in history to achieve the first winter ascent of an 8000-meter peak.

We finally arrived at advanced base camp, where we stopped to recover strength. We turned to look at the mountain, but the summit was already shrouded in clouds. We couldn't even make out the little dots that were Darek and Jacek, way up there.

After half an hour, Piotr and I decided to set out again, continuing our descent toward base camp, toward the end of our adventure and to the relative luxury of a softer sleeping pad, a cook, and a stove radiating heat.

Meanwhile, Darek and Jacek were starting their fight for survival. That night they reached the tent at 7400 meters in terrible weather conditions. We talked to them on the radio from base camp. It was already dark, and we heard the deafening noise of the tent fabric being pounded by the wind. They said they were afraid the tent would suddenly blow away. They had their clothes on inside their sleeping bags, ready to jump out if their shelter was destroyed. We encouraged them and assured them we would leave the radio on at all times, ready for any and all contact.

That night was a terrible one for our two friends, who fought with all their strength to endure while suspended over an abyss. The temperature had plunged below −50 degrees Celsius. With the wind chill, the cold must have been inhuman.

They held out. In the morning, they tried firing up the two stoves to boil some water so they could warm their hands and feet with the steam. Jacek gave himself an injection of heparin, a vasodilator, to increase the sensation of heat before putting his gloves, dry socks, and boots back on and starting the descent.

They rightly decided to give up their goal in order to aim for what had become the true summit—survival. They were magnificent. They managed to descend the mountain to advanced base camp in zero visibility. The fixed ropes were their lifeline and their sheer grit the essential ingredient for managing to pull through.

After more than sixteen years of failed attempts by all the strongest mountaineers of that time, finally a new chapter in the story of winter exploration above 8000 meters had begun. For me, that summit represented eight years of waiting and a career's worth of plans.

For the eighth time, the Polish had been among the key players in the first winter ascent of an 8000er. For the first time, someone who wasn't Polish also managed to make this dream come true—an Italian.

THAT SHISHAPANGMA CLIMB SHUFFLED THE cards quite a bit. It was a surprise. It reignited interest in winter ascents and removed the shroud of skepticism. Last but not least, it made the multitude of hardened critics—who, from time immemorial, have squandered their precious existence judging the lives of others—gnash their teeth.

I've stubbornly tried, not always successfully, to uphold the principle of doing a sort of mountaineering that's not doomed to clone the experiences of others. For me, Shishapangma was the confirmation and affirmation of that principle. I hadn't set out to "collect" the 8000ers. Nor had I chosen advantageous objectives with a high likelihood of success. That's not my kind of mountaineering. Though I respect it fully and completely, that approach wouldn't hold the power to motivate me through all the struggles, the decisions, the sacrifices demanded by the vertical world. The (overused) words "adventure" and "exploration" are the foundations on which I have built my approach to mountaineering. Sometimes, I find myself repeating the typical route on an 8000er in the usual season. But that always leaves me with a sense of not having done anything exploratory or adventurous. I feel like a mere enthusiast, a high-altitude tourist. It is a success on the surface only, insignificant in the history of alpinism and human exploration. And I go home with my desires—for inquiry, for the unknown, for discovery—unfulfilled.

Alpinism is an art form, like painting or music. Just as there are those who portray fantastic landscapes on canvas and write extraordinary scores, there are also those who attempt to venture into different territory—the territory of innovation, a more complicated and perhaps less readily understood form of art. Nevertheless, each form has its dignity. For that reason, I don't judge or criticize any style of mountaineering, not even the commercial one based on Sherpas, oxygen, and fixed ropes from start to finish. That would be an arrogant attitude, one seriously lacking in respect.

With equal lucidity and objectivity, however, I don't ignore the difference between one climb and another. I was inspired by alpinism as done by history's greats, those who are universally recognized as the historical elite, such as Cassin, Bonatti, and Messner. (I'm citing only my fellow Italians here, but I have had many other role models of diverse nationalities.) At their most authentic core, they all shared the same desires: to explore the mountains and, above all, themselves; to face the unknown; to push their limits; to satisfy their hunger for knowledge. These qualities are commonly found among the greats of science, medicine, literature, art, and also of exploration. When I think of Marco Polo, or Christopher Columbus, I think of explorers who walked into the unknown. The names Galileo, Michelangelo, Leonardo evoke the thirst to know, to explore, to not take anything for granted.

That's why I can't imagine myself climbing the fixed ropes of the usual route on the umpteenth climb of an 8000er during the most favorable season. Maybe I could do it if I worked as an alpine guide, or to acclimatize for an upcoming alpine-style climb. I'd definitely have trouble on those kinds of fixed ropes. Maybe I would still be happy and satisfied at the top, but I wouldn't be any closer to living out my greatest dream, my inspiration, and my way of life: to venture beyond the tracks left by my greatest teachers.

The way I practice alpinism is the fruit of a love affair, a genuine romantic passion for that which moved me, captured my imagination, and made me accept the risks that this love entails. That's the real reason I love doing winter ascents and new routes, and traversing and connecting mountains. Because for me this form of alpinism is not about success or setting records or performance. It's about experiencing the exploratory and adventurous aspect of things. It's the pursuit of what enchanted me, what made me happy. One doesn't ask "why" of love. And when you're in love, you don't behave according to convenience. It's a matter of powerful and irrational impulse.

What I don't want, though, is for this love to be blind and deaf. The same goes for the ambition that arises from such feeling. For that reason, I have always accepted my limits. Whenever it has become clear that this love could lead me beyond, into oblivion, I have always been able to back off. I have therefore "failed" a considerable number of times, precisely to ensure that a given adventure would not be my last. I have said "stop" and turned back, 250 meters, 160 meters, even as little as 90 meters from a summit. This fact has supplied the jackals and the idiots with ample ammunition to attack me, to trumpet and celebrate each failure, but I have never been ashamed of my decisions. Knowing when to stop isn't for wimps. It's for professionals, in the Alps and the Himalaya just as it is in the streets and nightclubs. I must write the script for my own life. It cannot be a clone or a performance of someone else's experiences.

My alpinism has been much like an original film. It might not be well received, but it's not the umpteenth remake of a well-known opera either. I have decided to shout my love from the rooftops, to tell its stories, to share it with others, with those who are interested in reading and hearing real accounts of alpinism without the hot air or heroics and what have you. The choice to share it "live"—that is, not as postmortem upon return from the climb but, rather, as the expedition unfolds—has further distinguished my approach to the vertical world, thereby deepening the rift between those who show interest and those who loudly express their disdain.

JANUARY 18, 2012

Scouting and acclimatization between Nanga
Parbat base camp (4230 m) and between
Camps 1 and 2 (5555 m)

TODAY WE WENT BACK UP. We've put up the tent at 5555
meters. We've been able to put our sleeping bags out to dry,
taking advantage of the sunshine. They were frozen.

It hasn't been easy to get here, on the glacier that leads
up to the col between Nanga Parbat and Ganalo Peak, but
we hope it's been another important step forward. I actually think we've already located the beginning of the route
opened by Reinhold Messner and Hans Peter Eisendle
in 2000. We also found some old gear that might have
belonged to their expedition or one of the following.

CHAPTER 5

THE COURAGE TO TURN BACK

(BROAD PEAK)

AFTER SHISHAPANGMA, I STAYED HOME to enjoy the following winter in the Alps while working on the project I later completed in the spring of 2006: a solo traverse of Everest, going south to north from Nepal to Tibet via the highest mountain on the planet. Although I used oxygen for three hours and climbed via the typical routes, it was still an adventure in every sense of the word because a climb with descent via the opposite face had never been done before on Everest. Naturally, I am thinking of reattempting the same challenge soon without oxygen, with some variations on the theme.

At the end of 2006, however, I felt the pull toward a winter ascent with a historical and exploratory flavor. A new dream began to take shape, giving me something to believe in and work toward. After Shishapangma, six 8000-meter summits remained unscaled in winter: one in Nepal (Makalu) and five in Pakistan (Nanga Parbat, Gasherbrum I and II, Broad Peak, and K2.)

Despite twenty years' worth of attempts, no one had ever summited an 8000-meter peak in Pakistan in winter. This fact intrigued me quite a lot. What's more, I was inspired by the thought of surpassing this human limit, of breaching this exploratory boundary for the first time.

Everyone at that time was saying that the Karakoram (though Nanga Parbat is technically part of the Himalaya) was much more severe than the Himalaya, nearly inhuman in comparison. In short, winter ascents in Pakistan were judged virtually impossible. Of course, that only ignited and stoked my desire to try it, to experience this alpine frontier firsthand. They said that Everest without supplemental oxygen was an impossible undertaking too. Then came Reinhold Messner, another controversial and criticized mountaineer, who shut everyone up by going beyond commonly accepted human limitations. As with Christopher Columbus, who ventured beyond the edge of the known world, Messner was mocked before leaving and praised upon his return, and his feats are still remembered today.

This is how I came to organize a winter expedition to Broad Peak, with departure after December 21, 2006, and deadline set for March 21, 2007. I didn't want to "win" at all costs, and so no big team, no oxygen, no Sherpas or high-altitude porters—instead, a light-and-lean exploration on one of Pakistan's giants. I had already climbed Broad Peak in 2003, nonstop from base camp in twenty-four hours, and so I was very familiar with it. I knew it wasn't a particularly dangerous mountain. But I also knew it had been attempted over and over in winter without success, and from reports and articles on previous expeditions I sensed the extraordinary ferocity of winter in the Karakoram.

Reading more in-depth about the history of Himalayan mountaineering, I was struck by the fact that it's always been Western climbers who've taken credit for conquering the world's highest peaks—with the exception of Everest, where it was the Sherpa Tenzing Norgay who deservedly starred in that memorable moment of his home's alpine history. Aside from him, no non-Westerner is mentioned, despite several notable instances. Take, for example, the case of Mahdi, a Hunza who bivied with Bonatti on K2 at 8000 meters and is rarely given due credit. (The Hunza are the inhabitants of the Hunza, Nagar, and Yasin valleys of northern Pakistan.)

As for winter mountaineering on 8000ers, there wasn't a single non-Western climber noted. For that reason, I thought that a Pakistani should write the first page on winter exploration of his mountains. So I decided to ask Shaheen Baig to accompany me on the expedition. A strong mountaineer, he had already climbed K2 and other prestigious mountains in his own country. We'd been introduced by Ashraf Aman, a longtime friend and the owner of Adventure Tour Pakistan, to whom I'd entrusted organizational responsibility.

Shaheen would be a key player, sharing exactly 50 percent of not only the work but also the credit, images, and story of the attempt. No one would ever use him as a high-altitude porter, or worse, as a kind of pack horse, as sometimes happens even on noncommercial expeditions. He would be tied in to the other end of my rope.

We flew to Broad Peak base camp by helicopter, since the porters had declared it impossible to cover the entire Baltoro Glacier on foot, which is the classic approach for a summer trek of six days. We had two other Pakistanis with us, a cook named Didar Ali and a base-camp manager and handyman, Amin Mohammet. They had both been with me on previous expeditions in Pakistan, and our relationships were tried and true.

The expedition immediately had to contend with the meteorological and environmental realities of the Karakoram. We battled for two months on Broad Peak (8047 m), K2's neighbor across the way, using all the energy and solutions at our disposal. We awaited good weather for weeks at a time. In the few hours granted us, we tried to climb as much as possible and set up the camps, but then we'd get literally thrown to the ground by hurricane-like winds and besieged by weather fronts akin to divine punishment. And still we held out, until provisions and stove fuel started to run out.

Staying there for another two months was both test and confirmation of just how strong my motivation for that type of climb was. I could have found thousands of reasons and excuses to run back home and put an end to that extreme physical and mental struggle. But I didn't. Actually, I would have stayed longer if I could have, in spite of being the only foreigner on the team.

During the entire expedition I documented everything daily on my blog, complete with high-def images from my camera. Canon was my technical sponsor for images and communications, and I kept its staff constantly up-to-date. A three- or four-minute video, shot to capture the climb or our daily routine as we waited, became the means of giving others an appreciation for what a winter ascent actually involves.

We only got to 6900 meters during that attempt of 2006–7. I went home with knowledge and experience that would serve me very well in the future. I had gotten within 1100 meters of the summit, still quite far off, but I had endured and battled terrible conditions for a very long time. I returned without frostbite. I wasn't demoralized. Instead, I was more conscious of my potential and the difficulties of that kind of climb.

I reflected on that expedition at length, analyzing it and noting its faults and merits. It didn't take me long to recharge, get back into shape, and plan the next goal. In fact, at the end of that same year I set out again for another attempt on Broad Peak.

The only change from the previous year was the team. I invited an Italian friend from Anterivo in the South Tyrol, Leonhard Werth, as photographer and base-camp support. I also extended an invitation to another Pakistani, Qudrat Ali, who had already climbed four of the five 8000ers in Pakistan and was like a brother to Shaheen. Didar and Amin were once again cook and assistant cook.

We left near Christmas (after the obligatory December 21 start of winter) and reached Islamabad during the night. It was colder than the previous year. The city was heavily guarded, of course, with checkpoints everywhere. The interior and undercarriage of every vehicle were inspected, even the idling engine. When it became clear that we were Westerners, the procedures were somewhat accelerated.

Two days later, we flew over Nanga Parbat to Skardu on Pakistan International Airlines. We landed safely on a runway in the middle of an alluvial plain that the Indus River had created over millennia. Mountains of up to 5000 meters encircled us. There was a little bit of snow. The few people waiting outside the airport had only blankets to shield themselves from the biting cold. The Adventure Tour Pakistan operators came in a jeep and took us downtown to the only hotel that was open and functional during the winter.

In the following days, Leonhard started to feel unwell. He had dysentery and stomach pain, probably due to a food-borne, drug-resistant bug. The porters gave no guarantee that they would make it all the way, and they wanted four times the summer salary—and rightly so. Also, they hinted that in the event of a storm (which was likely), they would ditch everything on the glacier. All things considered, flying in was more cost effective, so we decided to take a helicopter to base camp.

We waited another twenty days for the soldiers to fly us to base camp. The delay wasn't their fault. The fault lay with Askari Aviation, a well-known and unreliable business. For years, this monopoly has been making a profit from exploiting requests for helicopter use, even for rescues. The company acts as intermediary between those who need the service and the soldiers who actually do the flying. This business is made up of retired officials who clearly run the situation to suit themselves and generally ask for quadruple what they pay the soldiers. It would be a blessing for Pakistan, and for tourism throughout the country, if the business was confronted and closed, but its political and military connections make this almost impossible.

While we waited, we did many acclimatizing climbs on the surrounding mountains, including overnights above 4000 meters. Leo wasn't improving. In fact, he was getting weaker and weaker, so I decided to make him return to Italy while it was still possible. Evacuating him once on the glacier would have been next to impossible and very expensive, assuming there was even a helicopter available to take him out.

So there were three of us left—Qudrat, Shaheen, and me—facing a wait that seemed to go on forever.

At long last, Major Faraq, official of the Skardu helicopter team, took the controls of the Mi-17, a Russian-made flying machine used by militaries in almost every part the world. We flew to base camp with the entire load of supplies stowed inside the aircraft.

From there, the load needed to be distributed over several trips in order to ensure safe operation of the helicopter. First, a trip to Paju at 3500 meters, to the base of the Baltoro Glacier; then two trips to base camp. The lower density of high-alpine air affects the helicopter a lot, reducing its performance by as much as 80 percent compared to sea level, depending on the temperature, humidity, and altitude.

Faraq did an extraordinary job of organizing the transport of all the supplies. He loaded half into the helicopter and hooked the other half to the external central cable. He dropped us along with some of our gear on the first trip. Then he circled twice over that spot. He did the first pass at reduced speed, slow enough to avoid getting sucked into his own vortex, and unhooked the load just a few meters from the ground. At the end of the second pass, he set down on the pad we'd hastily prepared and unloaded all the rest. The air displaced by the main rotor churned up the snow and intensified the cold. Our hands were ice cold within minutes. Some procedures could not be done with gloves on, so it was a relief when the helicopter started hovering and took off valley-ward toward Concordia, skimming over the glacier as it lifted off.

A surreal, frozen silence settled around us, broken only by the wind. We got moving right away. It was already past noon and we still hadn't set up the tent, our haven.

Base camp was completely set up in little more than two days. To shelter ourselves from the awful gusts of wind that were sure to arrive, we positioned our camp in a hollow, almost a hole in the glacier. I remembered those winds well from the previous winter.

The current expedition was a real battle, with umpteen exhausting inter-vals of fast climbs up the mountain and quasi-epic, hasty descents to base camp, all done in forbidding weather conditions and hurricane-like winds. Once again, I decided to share it all "live," via the same blog as on our prior attempt. I documented each day with pictures of what we were experiencing and what we were attempting to achieve.

I was in almost daily contact with my trusted meteorologist Karl Gabl, a veritable forecasting guru who lives and works in Innsbruck. He's also a mountain guide and a man of unparalleled expertise. In his messages, certain words repeated almost without variation: wind, cloud, wind, snow, more wind.

Pushing our pace and gritting our teeth, we managed to set up Camp 1, and then Camp 2 at 6400 meters. We also got up to 6600 meters and fixed some rope. When March arrived, I asked for special permission to stay at base camp so I could keep trying until the bitter end, right up until the spring equinox if necessary. The government gave us only ten more days because, strangely, according to the Ministry of Tourism's bureaucracy, February 28 marks the end of winter.

Shaheen and Qudrat were surprised to see me so determined. They even asked me if perhaps it wasn't time to wrap up the expedition.

The cook later told me he'd seen them near tears at the mere idea of staying another ten days on that glacier. And it wasn't a question of gear. Their boots, clothing, sleeping bags, gloves, ice axes, and crampons were all identical to mine, top-quality gear, indispensable for survival in those conditions. The real weak spot in this kind of expedition is the mind, and it is exactly there that the first cracks appear. Shaheen and Qudrat were amazing, and still are, but maybe they had a lower tolerance threshold. I have never claimed to be better or stronger than others. Quite the contrary. I likely just have greater determination and tolerance for suffering. I didn't want to back down. The time came for the last possible attempt before our obligatory departure. Karl's forecast showed three days of alternating clear weather and blizzards. We decided to seize that last window of acceptable weather and set off.

We arrived at Camp 2 in just a few hours. The good weather started to turn in the last hour of the climb and severely tested us throughout our night up there. By the next morning, the wind had died down somewhat and we started to climb. We were loaded down with ropes, sleeping bags, camp stoves, food, and a small tent. Our intention was to establish Camp 3 at 7000 meters—an altitude not yet reached, even by me the previous year. After a few hours the sun came out and lifted our spirits. We continued over a slab of hard ice that led between some rocks. Then, suddenly, a dark cloud descended and we were shrouded in fog. It was probably still windy and clear elsewhere; but where we were, the mountain was cloaked in cloud. We were opposite a sloping plateau that rose directly to another, more level one. We put a few flags in the snow, knowing we could easily get lost if the fog got thicker or a snowstorm blew in.

We continued, staying roped and taking thirty steps between rests. We took turns leading and breaking trail. At a certain point we came across an abandoned tent, probably from the previous summer. I identified it as Russian by its tunnel shape and green color. Snow had accumulated around this light structure, providing shelter from the wind. We put our small tent in the lee of this formation and immediately jumped inside. We were at 7000 meters. It was terribly cold and our high-altitude suits were totally iced up at the collar. We were wearing full neoprene face masks, too, with only holes for the eyes and tiny perforations over the mouth.

Although satisfied by our accomplishment, we were far from the relative security of base camp and totally exposed to high-altitude winds. Via satellite phone, Karl announced an unexpected day of good weather. The temperatures would be very low, with 70-kilometer-per-hour winds, but it was the best news we could have had. I told my two tentmates right away. We decided to attempt the summit but not to leave before six. Any earlier and it would be too cold and we wouldn't last more than a few minutes. What's more, in the near dark we wouldn't be able to make out the best route toward the col on Broad Peak at 7840 meters, and from there the ridge to the foresummit and then the actual summit at 8047 meters.

Wearing our high-altitude suits and boot liners inside our sleeping bags, we lay tightly together in an attempt to warm each other and retain every precious bit of body heat. Despite these measures, the cold forced us to stay awake and mobile.

Finally it was time to go. I went first, followed by Shaheen and, lastly, Qudrat. The snow was lying in drifts. During some stretches it bore my weight. In others, I plunged in to the knee so our pace wasn't exactly fast and even, and the conditions winded us. The cold was striking, so we did our best to wiggle our fingers and toes constantly inside our gloves and boots.

At a certain point, a large crevasse barred the way. I turned and saw Shaheen 50 meters below me. Another 50 meters below him was Qudrat, who was shaking his head and banging his boots together, trying to get his circulation going. I shouted a warning about the crevasse and my intention to go around it or find an ice bridge across it.

Qudrat gestured that he would stop climbing and return to the tent. He couldn't feel his feet and knew full well the serious risk of irreversible frostbite. I gave him the thumbs-up and then concentrated on finding a way past that frightening chasm. I trudged back and forth for an hour until I glimpsed a bridge spanning the crevasse. I checked the condition of the bridge with my ax while I waited for Shaheen. It seemed solid and supportive. I tied in to one end of the rope and asked Shaheen to belay me. I tried to walk lightly, delicately, as though on eggshells or a scrap of silk. I was suspended above a deep, dark crevasse and each second seemed to last forever. Then, at last, I found myself on the other side.

Shaheen joined me. We put the rope back in the pack and continued our trek, each at his own pace, along the increasingly steep slope toward the col. With the sun shining on us, we continued slowly but relentlessly upward. We had lost all sense of the passage of time. I had no idea what time of day it was: glancing at that section of the altimeter would involve taking off my gloves and peeling back the cuffs of several garments I was wearing beneath my high-altitude suit.

Shaheen was falling behind. He was already 150 meters away. I often saw him sitting on the snow. But he didn't want to give up, either. And he didn't want to leave me alone. All he wanted was to follow me.

I found some old fixed ropes in the final couloir. Some were usable, others just pieces. By now I was on all fours. This lessened my exposure to the wind, which had been increasing in velocity for a few hours. Shaheen fell farther and farther behind.

At one point, I saw the col at 7840 meters, the famous "door" to the final ridge of Broad Peak. I turned to see my partner once again seated on the snow, with head resting on ice ax. I decided to check the time in order to calculate how much time was required to get to the summit and back. I had to get a picture of the situation.

I quickly took off my glove, messily hiked up everything covering my altimeter, and looked at the time: 2:26 p.m.

"No, fuck no! It can't be that late!"

The sun was in fact already well in the west, toward the ridgeline. Looking upward, I could make out the foresummit. It was close, but getting to the summit would require another hour and a half, at which point it would be 4:00 p.m. What would I do on the threshold of a winter night, once I was on the summit? And what about Shaheen?

"This can't be happening. Not like this . . . it can't finish like this . . . "

I looked down at my partner. He got up, took eight or ten steps, and then threw himself to the ground once again.

"We'll both die like this," I told myself. "Go down, Simone. That's it, it's over. Get moving and head down."

It was my conscience talking, guiding me. I turned for a last look. The summit was sunlit against a perfectly clear sky. Just an occasional wind gust now and then. The moment seemed perfect for claiming our victory, but also for choosing to live, before it was too late.

I don't know whether it was tears or spindrift in my eyes, but I recall my vision was blurred.

I started down, gaining speed and agility as I lost altitude. I reached Shaheen and told him his struggle was over.

"Get up, Shaheen, we'll go down together. We'll go back to Qudrat. He'll have made us some tea."

Going back down was just as hard for Shaheen. He often collapsed onto the ground, and this worried me more than a little. Pushing on and producing body heat had exhausted his energy.

We got to the ice bridge, crossed it, and labored toward the tent. We got there around four. Qudrat had in fact made tea. He had kept us in sight and seen everything, so he didn't ask questions. After some swallows of tea, he asked what I thought we should do.

"Listen. Shaheen is already very tired," I told him. "If he sleeps up here, tomorrow he won't get up. The weather forecast is for it to get worse tomorrow and we're too high up. You're more rested than me. Stay with him, make sure he drinks, then take the tent and start down for Camp 2. I'll take everything else and go ahead of you. I'll wait for you with some food and tea, okay? It's almost all fixed ropes from here and we have the route markers, so you can't get lost. Keep the radio on. Keep moving toward the bottom. I'll wait for you. If it gets dark, I'll send light signals. The sky is clear and the moon will light everything up for a few hours before the bad weather hits."

"Okay, Simone. Thanks. See you later."

I set out again. The descent was fast, facilitated by the more compact snow and fixed ropes. On the steeper sections, I used a figure-8 to lower myself. When it was less steep, I just used a carabiner and rappeled.

The more altitude I lost, the more I could feel the oxygen level increasing and the sensation of cold diminishing. I was almost obsessed with the idea of getting down quickly and went faster than expected. When I got to Camp 2, there was still some light. I got into the tent and took a deep breath. I laid down and closed my eyes just for a minute or so before I got moving again without further delay. I filled the little pot with snow and fired up the stove. I peeked out, squinting upward, and saw two headlamps. Good. That was my two friends. Shaheen had probably rallied thanks to the tea and the companionship of his close friend. The increase in oxygen as they lost altitude had done the rest. They reached the tent after about an hour, shattered but safe.

All three of us kept our clothes on inside our sleeping bags and slept well enough. I changed my socks and put the used ones inside my suit to warm and dry them in my armpits.

As Karl had predicted, with morning came a snowstorm, so savage it seemed intent on ripping us off the mountain. The wind forced the tent fabric to cling to us, making it a struggle just to have breakfast and drink something.

There was no time to waste. With one last push we could get to base camp, to shelter and safety. We had to. Once out of the tent, I loaded myself down with all the gear I could manage. Qudrat took most of the rest and Shaheen the last of it. He was doing better but certainly wasn't 100 percent. You could see it in his eyes. I started down only once my two friends had shouldered their packs and put on their crampons. The series of fixed ropes that lay between us and Camp 1 forced us to descend to 5400 meters one at a time. After that, we would be able to descend simultaneously, rappeling rather than hanging fully from the fixed ropes.

When they arrived at Camp 1, Shaheen was stumbling, but the most exposed section was behind us. We stopped in the shelter of a boulder for a few minutes. The wind was constant and there was even some sleet.

"Shaheen, how's it going?"

"Good, good *caco* [brother]," he replied.

"Hang in there, just stick it out. We'll be at base camp in two hours, maybe less."

This last part of the descent to the base of the face at 5200 meters was an ordeal for Shaheen. He fell again and again. Each time he was at risk of a deadly slide toward the valley. We helped him as much as we could, especially Qudrat, who urged me to stay 50 meters ahead and wait for them at every anchor point. The three of us were taking a mortal risk by hanging from a single fixed rope.

We radioed Didar and Amin at base camp, asking them to meet us with a thermos of very sweet tea and some cookies. Getting there seemed to take an eternity, especially for Shaheen, who was nearly dragging himself along by then.

After crossing one last exhausting boulder field and tongue of ice, we arrived at base camp near the end of the afternoon, and the end of our vertical adventure. Without a doubt, each of us, especially Shaheen, had explored the limits of our endurance and our tolerance for exertion, cold, and altitude.

I immediately contacted Ashraf Aman, head of the trekking agency in Islamabad, and asked him to arrange a helicopter for our return journey. He proved very capable of managing the difficulties of dealing with Askari Aviation, so capable that the helicopter arrived just two days later to take us to Skardu, with Major Faraq once again at the controls. That spare and desolate country seemed the most beautiful place on Earth.

A doctor attended to Shaheen right away, examining him and prescribing some medication. But that night Shaheen felt bad again, and the next day we took him to the hospital (if you can call it that). He was admitted and treated for a full week, after which he was considered stable and was discharged. His vital signs had been hovering right on the edge, a sign that he'd truly given Broad Peak his all.

The time came to say good-bye and part company. Shaheen would head back to the Hunza via jeep and continue to his home in Shimshal. I would fly to Italy via Islamabad. It was a simple but heartfelt farewell. We all hugged, promising to stay in touch and breathe life into the youth mountaineering school in the Shimshal Valley. Shaheen, Qudrat, and many of the strongest high-altitude porters of Pakistan come from the Shimshal. I also thanked and said good-bye to Didar and Amin. I tipped all four of them well, got into the minivan, and was off to the airport.

It was March 17 when I boarded my flight home. Almost three months had passed since the start of my adventure. I'd had two Pakistanis for climbing partners and the Karakoram winter for my daily living environment. I hadn't managed to get to the Broad Peak summit, so I'd have to file the expedition away as another failure.

Yet this expedition had been a validation, a powerful experience from which I gleaned more certainty than uncertainty. I now knew that the deed could be done. It wasn't "impossible." Getting within 200 meters of the summit with such a small team in such extreme conditions had driven home that I wasn't taking a losing gamble, I wasn't just dreaming. I actually had the ability and the experience necessary for another winter climb above 8000 meters. I was ready to build a triumph upon this seeming defeat.

JANUARY 19, 2012
Nanga Parbat base camp (4230 m),
approximately -18°C and snowing

WE WERE HAPPY TO HAVE gotten this far yesterday, navigating the glacier by instinct, snowshoeing a little, then putting on crampons, then back to the snowshoes.

Then Matteo gave us upsetting news from base camp. This morning, we lost a great alpinist, but more importantly a friend, Mario Merelli. Mario had done it all, even 8000ers, and yet he met his end on the mountain he knew best, right above his home. There are no words. The news was a shock because both Denis and I were longtime friends of Mario's.

Today's plan was to climb to our Camp 3 at 6600 meters, stay overnight, and then go down to base camp. But we've decided to temporarily interrupt our climb and head down.

CHAPTER 6

BEKA BRAKAI CHHOK: THE BEAUTIFUL ONE

I WENT BACK TO PAKISTAN a few months later. It was summer, the "normal" season, with the usual high number of alpine expeditions going on. My project was decidedly less ordinary. The five 8000ers of that country are notoriously popular for their beauty and prestige, but I wasn't aiming for any of those. Rather, I planned to journey through a little-known and rarely visited valley near the border with Afghanistan. When I had put up a new route on Batokshi Peak (6050 m) in 2005, I had become familiar with the Batura Valley. There, hundreds of unclimbed and often unnamed peaks were just waiting to be explored.

Contrary to my usual pattern, I didn't have an Eastern European climbing partner on this expedition. Instead, I went for a Westerner. I have many Italian, European, and overseas climbing friends, but with this man, the bond goes beyond friendship. We trust each other. When it comes to our way of setting goals and our take on alpinism, we're on the same wavelength. I'm speaking of Hervé Barmasse, son of Marco

Barmasse. Marco was on my very first Everest expedition in 1992. He is one of the nicest people I've had the fortune of meeting, and he passed all of his best qualities on to Hervé: strength, generosity, humility, and incredible drive.

Our objective for summer 2008 was the 6940-meter peak of Beka Brakai Chhok. Some maps show it exceeding 7000 meters. Though measurements of its altitude varied, the essence of the mountain remained unchanged—very beautiful and unconquered, despite three previous attempts. The most recent attempt had ended 1000 meters from the summit after six days of climbing.

We acclimatized on Batokshi Peak, climbing during the day and sleeping on the top. From the summit we could see a lineup of climbers who were attempting the as-yet-unclimbed Batura II (7762 m). We had initially considered making an alpine-style ascent of that mountain, but knowing we'd find ourselves sharing the same face and route with a multimember team, we'd changed our minds and focused on Beka Brakai Chhok instead.

Back at base camp, which had been set up by the staff of Hunza Guides Pakistan, we rested, waiting for favorable weather conditions before heading to the base of the face at around 4800 meters. Once our little tent was set up, we readied ourselves for a speedy attempt. Despite the history of previous ascents and the undeniable challenges of the mountain, we decided for a nonstop round-trip, taking only the absolutely necessary gear. No tent, no sleeping bag, and no stove or sleeping mat either . . . nothing. Just a pack for each of us, 60 meters of 5-millimeter Dyneema rope plus another very thin Kevlar rope, a few ice screws, and two ice axes each.

We left at night and climbed as quickly as possible to 6000 meters, the highest point reached previously in multiple days of climbing. There, a knife-edged snowy ridge necessitated a long, delicate, and dangerous traverse toward the shoulder of Beka. Getting the better of that lofty traverse took us a number of precious hours and, once it was finally behind us, we realized we'd never be able to reach the top while it was still light. We bivouacked with nothing at 6200 meters, huddled together beneath a serac at the mouth of a crevasse. Obviously, we didn't sleep, given how busy we were massaging the tips of our fingers and toes to avoid frostbite.

When day broke at last, it was sunny. It wasn't long before we felt the benefit of those rays, and we went on with our climb. The snow was getting progressively, imperceptibly deeper, and progress became more and more demanding. We got to a complicated section of mixed climbing, which Hervé completed nimbly in two pitches, after which we could see the summit.

Then it was my turn to break trail on that infinite white expanse. I was breathless from exertion and altitude. I plunged in waist-deep with every step. The summit seemed to be actively repelling us, but at that point we were too close for the notion of giving up to even cross our minds. The weather was perfect, with blue sky and minimal wind. I called upon all of my physical and mental strength to go on, staying roped in, always careful not to slip. We were walking on the edge of a knife but the summit was so close, only a few hellish steps away.

When I finally managed to haul myself upright onto the snowcapped peak of Beka, I nearly exploded with joy. I turned and signaled Hervé, who joined me within moments. What I remember best about that climb was our powerful handshake. We took a few pictures and shot some video, and then we were off on our long descent. We hadn't so much as touched food or water in more than twenty-four hours.

The descent was just as complicated and quasi-epic, but we made it. Forty-three hours after our departure, we were back at base camp with the first ascent of Beka Brakai Chhok in the bag.

It was an exciting and satisfying climb. Even though not done in winter, it proved very useful for future winter climbs. Our "fast and light" approach led me to believe that adopting that style for an 8000-meter peak could increase our chance of success, especially in winter, when the windows of good weather are notoriously small and rare.

Before going home, however, I had a promise to keep with Qudrat and Shaheen. Hervé and I went to the Shimshal Valley to visit the mountaineering school, just as I'd said I would after Broad Peak. The school had been opened in the interim. Thanks to The North Face, we'd begun to support it.

The idea of founding a mountaineering school in Pakistan—open to both boys and girls—was hatched during the first of our two winter experiences on Broad Peak. Then, during the last one, when Qudrat and Shaheen had stayed with me for more than two months, we brainstormed the foundations for the project more seriously. I had promised my personal support and also that of my sponsors, who have always shown their concern for the inhabitants of mountains and other remote areas by supporting humanitarian projects.

I want to give happiness back to those who've given me happiness. This desire first arose some years ago, when I initiated the construction of a new school serving 396 children in the isolated village of Syadul, Nepal. After a promising start, problems with the Maoists slowed the work and increased costs. Fortunately, the Rotary Club of Bergamo West gave us a considerable hand, and the school was finished. After that, I began financing the educational expenses of three children in difficult circumstances. We're talking about a paltry sum, maybe a few hundred Euros a year, an amount I hardly miss, but it changes their lives a lot.

After these small efforts in Nepal, I very much wanted to try to do something in Pakistan, a difficult country and one so different from mine. Shaheen and Qudrat were the right partners. I had complete confidence in them, and they had demonstrated a much broader mentality than is commonly found in Islamic countries. An alpine school for both boys *and* girls together, in Shimshal, seemed to me a very grandiose and courageous idea, almost like another winter ascent of Broad Peak.

The school was to be called Shimshal Mountaineering School (SMS). Qudrat and Shaheen had discussed it with the local nambardar, a prominent elder of acknowledged charisma who fulfills the functions of mayor, lawyer, and notary and whose word is law. With his approval, we set up meetings with the parents of twenty boys and ten girls to explain the proposed project and our goals. Within a few months the school was in operation, the only one of its kind in Pakistan. Classes had begun. I stayed in constant contact with Qudrat and Shaheen. They were the first and only instructors at the school, offering their many years of expedition experience.

Meanwhile, I had started sowing seeds in Italy as well and was finding fertile ground. The North Face, for example, arranged for a shipment of technical apparel for all the students at SMS. In addition, I had promised to give some theoretical and practical classes, as well as to recruit other professional friends to the project. So in the end, when it came to the SMS students, the Broad Peak "failure" was becoming "Summit: Accomplished."

Hervé was my first choice of guest instructor and he was enthusiastic. We met up with Qudrat and Shaheen in Aliabad in the Hunza Valley. From there we went to Shimshal by jeep. The area had become accessible to vehicles only recently. The road's construction started in 1986 and finished in 2003. The work was done using only local labor, with tools such as shovels, pickaxes, and in some sections, explosives. For thousands of years before that, Shimshal had been accessible only on foot, three days' walk along the nearest road, through narrow canyons and steep slopes.

Our jeep squeezed through a canyon along what seemed more like a wide hiking trail than a road for four-wheel drives. We gradually gained altitude. The village named Shimshal lies at 3200 meters. Shimshal Pass, the highest point in the region, is at 4735 meters. On the other side of that pass is China. Before the road's construction, the shepherds of this area found it much faster and more convenient to go to China to shop, especially in the summer.

After a few hours we reached the vivid, dream-like plain of Shimshal. People are friendly there. The women and men working in the fields or in the village don't hide away immediately at the sight of outsiders, nor do they show hostility at the intrusion with malevolent looks. They speak Wakhi, a language completely different from that of the neighboring areas only a few hours away.

Before reaching the village, Shaheen had his brother stop the jeep in front of a glacier overlooking the road. It led down from Distaghil Sar. At 7885 meters, this is the nineteenth-highest mountain in the world, summited only three times. The face visible from Shimshal is still unclimbed, and Qudrat pointed it out. It felt close enough to touch. The school's technical classes on glacier travel were held on the glacier just a few meters away from where we were standing.

At the time of our visit, things were delicate in Shimshal. There was something troubling in the wind, and Qudrat had warned us about it in the jeep during the trip there. There had been a tragedy during a K2 expedition and some of the victims were local high-altitude porters. To understand Shimshal's mountaineering tradition, it's important to keep in mind that more than two thousand of the region's inhabitants have been engaged as porters for high-altitude expeditions in the past sixty years. Many of them have climbed at least one 8000er. There's an extraordinary concentration of mountaineering experience in the valley. The incident on K2 threatened to wipe out this marvelous history because the surviving Western climbers had seen fit to blame the tragedy on the porters' lack of professionalism and competence rather than taking responsibility themselves. Therefore, the Western survivors were heroes, while those who were no longer around to defend themselves were held responsible.

Afterward, when questioned by the national and international media, I had the chance to give my opinion on the situation. I hadn't been there on K2, but the glaringly evident errors made during the climb were visible to all, especially to those who do high-altitude mountaineering. Although my opinion reflected that of the international mountaineering community, and even though I have emails, interviews, and testimonials to support it, I was harshly criticized for expressing my opinion. No one has ever brought action against me, though, a sign that those taken to task know they risk shooting themselves in the foot and winding up in a colossal mess. In life I've learned to apologize, to admit my mistakes and sift them for gold. That tragedy could have been a perfect occasion to do just that. A lesson could have been gleaned for all future mountaineers and climbers of K2, but those involved preferred to create false heroes and obscure the truth.

During my visit to Shimshal, many wives and children were grieving for their loved ones who were not only lost on K2 but unjustly accused as well. Hervé and I went to funeral rites in their homes, offering condolences on behalf of the international alpine community and apologies for what had been said by those involved. But those who really should have apologized were careful not to.

So it was a very difficult time to talk about mountaineering or a school, but these people's composure and forward-thinking were extraordinary. We met with all the students regardless, gave classes on theory, and showed some videos. Those were beautiful days. We struck a perfect balance between the commemoration of the newly dead and the determination of those who wanted to follow in their footsteps and go beyond, to a better life.

Today, three years later, the Shimshal school project is well established. Fineco Bank joined The North Face in contributing financially, funding construction of the brick building that houses the students and all their gear. At the school in Syadul, Nepal, we've also installed solar panels to provide heat. In the winter, at –20 degrees Celsius, children in this region usually study in frigid classrooms or outside in the sun to take advantage of its heat on the rare occasions when it shows up.

JANUARY 23, 2012
Nanga Parbat base camp (4230 m), -16°C

WE LEFT ITALY ALMOST A month ago and things are going well here on the whole. Today was to be the departure day for setting up the final camp, Camp 3 at 6600 meters, making it relatively permanent for two nights and maybe getting up to 7000 meters. We postponed all of that by a day because of a minor ailment. Last night I had some stomach problems. I ate nothing but plain rice with olive oil today. I'm doing well today, thank God, so we plan to leave tomorrow.

CHAPTER 7

MAKALU: THE GREAT BLACK ONE

AFTER THE WINTER EXPEDITION TO Broad Peak, the summer ascent of Beka Brakai Chhok, and the visit to Shimshal Mountaineering School, I was only home for the autumn of 2008. My winter experience ten months prior had very much motivated me to stick to my choice of winter mountaineering. I was ready to make my third attempt on Broad Peak and finish the job. Also, due to my expeditions and my success on Shishapangma, the race was back on for first winter ascents on the 8000ers. In fact, every year there were more departures during the cold season, with an increasing number of them starting after December 21. It might take a few more years yet, but I'm sure that eventually this rule (not made by me) of declaring the departure date will become the official norm to uphold.

In the winter of 2008–9, a Polish expedition announced its intention to take on Broad Peak. So after my two attempts, someone else had decided to try. The mountain didn't belong to me. I understood that perfectly. But I didn't want to find myself in the same base camp as another team vying for the same objective. That could easily have become a competition over how, where, and when to scale Broad Peak.

So I decided to pick another 8000er that hadn't been climbed in winter. I settled on Makalu, the last remaining Nepalese peak in that category. At 8500 meters, this mountain had been, absurdly, one of the first to be attempted in winter—by Renato Casarotto, Mario Curnis, and Romolo Nottaris in 1980. With that attempt, two Italians and a Swiss had joined the Polish in kick-starting winter mountaineering on 8000-meter peaks.

My dear friend Denis was once again my chosen climbing partner. I'd climbed with my Kazakhstani brother many times in many seasons, in the Himalaya, the Karakoram, the Pamir, and the Tien Shan. Denis didn't hesitate. All he needed to know was when we were leaving. He and I truly have a special connection, unparalleled. I love it when people talk about us as climbing partners, as a vertical duo, rather than focusing on the climbs we've done separately or alone. Together we're better. We achieve updated versions of what others have done in the past. By "others" I'm referring to the unforgettable founding duos of high-altitude mountaineering such as Messner and Kammerlander, Kukuczka and Wielicki, Loretan and Troillet, and very few others. I'd love it if our climbing together was remembered as the union of two personalities who were able to perfectly mesh in ability, character, and imagination to pursue a common dream. Sharing success is important. It's a cornerstone of life and coexistence.

The harmony I have with Denis is real. That's why it infuriates me when the usual idiotic, mean-spirited people think we've chosen to climb together out of mere convenience, or when someone maintains that one of us is carrying the other. Neither of us has ever done more, carried more, thought more, or initiated more than the other. When we climb together, it's fifty-fifty. Anything people say to the contrary is simply gossip fueled by spite, a sentiment more common in mountain-eering than in other disciplines, athletic or not.

Makalu was yet another of our shared dreams. Denis would never have accepted my invitation if he hadn't been attracted to and inspired by the prospect of an arduous alpine exploration, as I was.

Actually, Denis was particularly motivated to attempt the winter ascent of Makalu. He had tried the previous year and turned back at 7450 meters. The intensity of the wind and cold had astounded him. More than once, he'd felt close to being blown off the mountain, held back only by his climbing partners' rope. Nives Meroi, Romano Benet, and Luca Vuerich had tried to climb Makalu in winter that same year, but they too had been forced to give up due to terrible weather conditions.

I was familiar with Makalu as well. I'd been there way back in 1993 with Josef Rakoncaj's Czechoslovakian team. We'd tried the Kukuczka route. I'd reached 8300 meters, a little higher than my companions but still 163 meters from the summit. I'd been tired, exhausted in fact. I'd had enough energy in reserve to reach the summit but almost certainly wouldn't have had enough to get back to base camp alive.

For this new Makalu climb, I'd invited only Denis, no one else. I wanted just the two of us to do it, without high altitude climbers, oxygen, or other outside assistance. This approach might have seemed presumptuous, given that Makalu had been repelling every type of assault for almost thirty years. What's more, Denis and I were planning a fast alpine-style ascent, and that baffled people.

We left around Christmastime. I'd hired my friend Nima Nuru Sherpa, owner of Cho Oyu Trekking in Kathmandu, to take care of the logistics and red tape. My intention was to travel in two teams. Jagat Limbu, the cook, and the assistant cook, Mingma, would go immediately to the

Arun Valley at the foot of Makalu, on a small airline that would later take them to Tumlingtar with all the expedition supplies. They would then engage the necessary number of porters and start the twelve-day trek to base camp.

Denis and I would instead head to the Khumbu Valley to acclimatize on Island Peak. We would sleep on the summit (about 6200 m) to better adjust to the altitude. Only once completely acclimatized would we travel quickly to Makalu to await the first window of good weather before starting the climb.

Everything seemed to be going well. Our load had cleared customs; the various bundles had been prepared for the porters in Kathmandu; the trips had been arranged for both Jagat and Mingma to go ahead of us with the gear and for Denis and I to go to the Khumbu Valley to acclimatize. I'd left a satellite phone with Jagat, via which he gave me daily updates on each leg of their journey with the porters. The weather was good and the strong high-altitude winds weren't noticeable in the valley. Even the temperatures were livable.

Once we were in the Khumbu Valley at Namche Bazaar, the first problem presented itself. I'd gotten a satellite modem as a new way of sending data quickly. It wasn't working. It connected to the satellite but wouldn't let me upload photos, videos, emails, et cetera—a major hassle, and difficult to resolve. I spent a whole day on the phone with the satellite operators who eventually told me, "We think the modem we sent is defective. Sorry. We'll ship another one right away."

Evidently, they didn't realize where I was. I gave them Nima's address in Kathmandu anyway. I would pick up the modem once we had finished acclimatizing.

The Khumbu Valley was nearly deserted. Extremely popular with thousands of trekkers and tourists in summer and fall, the valley had now returned to life as usual: a few yaks transporting the last of the seasonal provisions, children playing in front of stone houses, women intent on carrying bundles of wood home, old folks sitting on the sun-drenched doorsteps, praying. And all of it surrounded by soaring peaks, silence, and peace.

A week later we arrived at Chhukung village (4790 m), up against the north face of Ama Dablam and beneath the famous south face of Lhotse. We stayed at our friend Lopsang Sherpa's lodge. We were the only guests. We meant to climb Chhukung Ri first (5555 m) and then Island Peak the next day (6189 m), staying overnight.

The first, smaller peak was a steady easy climb. There was no snow, it was windy, temperatures were frigid but not extreme. We were back in time for a late lunch. I had enough time to wash up, change clothes, and eat something at Lopsang's lodge. In late afternoon, I made my daily call to Jagat, who was proceeding toward Makalu base camp with the caravan of porters.

"Hi, Jagat, it's me. How's it going, where are you?"

"Hi, Simone." His voice sounded different and I sensed something was wrong. "Big problem. It's the porters. They refuse to continue. The wind has driven too much snow into the valley bottom. There's also some on the steep slopes that we'll have to go down in the dark. Some of them already abandoned their loads."

"Fuck. Did you try offering them more money?"

"Did it. Didn't change a thing."

"Listen. Offer them more money again anyhow. Ask them to pick their loads back up and at least take them back to Tashigaon, the last village you just passed. Okay? Listen, make sure you insist. If they abandon everything right where you are, in the middle of the forest, it means the expedition is over and I've lost everything."

"Okay, okay, I'll try. I better hang up right away or I won't be able to catch up to the porters who already started heading back. I'll call you later!"

I spent the next two hours with my heart in my throat, afraid Jagat wouldn't be able to fix the situation. I kept the phone on and rested it against a rock with the antenna pointed toward the satellite. At last, it rang.

"Everything's okay, Simone. I managed to convince them. But I have to give them a raise or a bonus, as you authorized. They wouldn't have come back without that."

"Yes, of course. That's great, Jagat! Well done! Where are you taking all the stuff now? Tashigaon?"

"Yes, that's right."

"Okay. Wait for me there. Try to arrange all the gear in a place somewhere close to a meadow or a field, any level spot in the terrain where a helicopter will have enough room to land. We've got to be in touch every day, as usual. Better go easy on the phone batteries. Keep them warm!"

The call had set me at ease. The expedition was safe for now, but I had a good many problems to solve. I was at Chhukung with Denis and needed to get down fast. But the porters who had moved our gear to Island Peak—my clothing, a generator, the computer, the cameras—had already left. They wouldn't be back for another week, as agreed. So now I had no way to bring all of that gear back with me. I shared my problem with Lopsang.

"I'll rent you my mare, if you want her," he offered. "Load the two biggest bags onto her back and lead her down on the rope, as though she were on a leash. The problem is, the colt can't be separated from his mother, so he'll follow you. And I'm sure the stallion will also want to go. In the end, you'll have three horses but only the mare will be of any use to you. You can't load anything onto the stallion, he gets crazy and bucks."

"Sounds good, Lopsang. I'll go as far as Namche Bazaar tomorrow. I'll definitely find some porters there to go to Lukla. Send your assistant cook with me. It'll only take him a few hours to get back here on the mare."

It seemed we'd resolved our first glitch. I called Nima Nuru in Kathmandu and explained my problem with the porters, giving advance notice of my need for a helicopter.

As usual, Nima gave me his all. He negotiated with the military's top brass to get permission for a charter helicopter to Tashigaon. From there, the Mi-17 would go to Makalu base camp. He also booked a flight to Kathmandu for me. I would depart two days later from Lukla, the last village along the trek to Everest equipped with a small airport served by standard airlines.

The next day we set out, me with the mare "on leash" and the rest of her family following behind, and Denis carrying the pack and taking pictures while poking fun at me. By nightfall we reached Namche Bazaar, the Sherpa village at 3500 meters. I unloaded the mare and arranged hay and water for all three horses. We went to Nima's lodge, Sherpaland, and indulged in a large supper. Two porters had been engaged for us in the meantime. The next day, they would take over carrying the loads.

We arrived in Lukla in early afternoon and took a room at the Himalayan Lodge. Nima's cousin Dawa, the owner of the lodge, gave us our tickets for the first flight out the following day.

We still had the problem of the nonfunctional satellite modem. The replacement hadn't yet arrived in Kathmandu. The dealer had shipped it from Italy and I was anxiously awaiting its arrival by the next day at the latest. It would be a serious drawback to fly in to Makalu base camp without a replacement communication device.

We took the first flight out of Lukla the next morning and got to Kathmandu before 9:00. Nima was waiting for us at the airport. All of the bureaucratic procedures for the helicopter had already been set in motion. It was important for us to visit the military hangar, he told us, and talk to the pilot and the others who would be part of the charter flight.

We stayed in the airport and walked a few hundred meters to the military zone. We entered it without incident, thanks to being with Nima. The pilot and copilot were standing beside the Mi-17, ready for a military mission. We introduced ourselves, trying to be as friendly as possible, but we hardly needed to bother—it turned out the pilot also spoke Russian, having received his type rating for that helicopter in the Ukraine. When I told him that I'd been at the controls of an Mi-17 for a few hours, the conversation became a chat between two old acquaintances. After about ten minutes, we broached the topic of our charter flight. The two soldiers would happily do it, only they didn't know exactly where Tashigaon was, nor the base camp. I reassured them that I knew the locations well and would guide them, no problem. They just had to call me into the cockpit as soon as the Arun Valley came into view.

Once that exchange wrapped up, I asked Nima if the modem had arrived. Nope. I was worried and called Italy. The company confirmed that the shipment had been made days before, but there was still no sign of it at Customs. We had a single day left before departure. We tried to track the package and discovered that, surprisingly, it had arrived in Kathmandu. We went back to Customs but the offices had just closed for the day. Unfortunately, no one was moved by the offers we made.

"Shit. Just you wait and see, Nima. Tomorrow we'll fly to Makalu without the modem. Meanwhile, it's just on the other side of that wall and I can't get at it thanks to the fucking bureaucrats!"

"Let's hope for fog tomorrow. That way the flight will be delayed and I'll manage to pick up the modem just in time."

"I hope so, I really hope so, but I think we're holding out for the impossible."

Next morning? Fog.

Bet you Nima performs miracles, I thought. Come on, come on, come on, keep hoping, cross your fingers. At 7:30, we were at the airport with the soldiers, ready to leave as arranged.

"Sorry, Simone. It's too foggy. We have to wait."

"Yes, of course, no problem. We can leave as late as ten if you want."

"I have to leave as soon as possible. It's a long flight. And I need the better lift of colder morning temperatures to move your whole load to base camp. As soon as the fog clears, we take off. Stay here, ready to go."

Let's hope the fog doesn't lift before 9:30, I thought. Customs opens at 9:00, so Nima would be in time to claim the modem.

After a quarter of an hour, the blanket of fog slowly started to lift. I started to explain that an important package might have arrived for me, but the pilot silenced me immediately, saying the mission couldn't be held up. The two trips to base camp plus the break to service the helicopter would require a whole day. And they had to get back to Kathmandu before the clouds reduced visibility, compromising safety.

Nevertheless, I kept on hoping.

"Get on board, Simone. We're leaving. The control tower has authorized departure. Visibility is adequate—150 meters up, the fog is dispersing and it's clear."

I looked at my watch: 9:02.

"Fuck no, what bad luck!"

Nima had sent a man who knew the bosses in the various Customs offices well. We called him on the cell.

"So? Do you have it?"

"Not yet! They're still looking."

"Too late. Simone is about to take off."

Nima looked me in the eye and said, "Simone, don't worry about it. I'll send a porter with the modem. He'll get there, you can be sure of it, whether or not it snows. I'll outfit him with everything he needs. Just relax."

I've always trusted Nima like a brother because he's a man of his word. The fact that his business in Nepal hasn't had a single customer complaint in more than twenty years of operation is not by chance. In other words, he's first-rate. Together, we've now opened a tourism agency in Bergamo.

The helicopter was already on the pad. There was no time to waste. The two turbines roared into motion with their two-thousand-plus horse-power each. Denis and I got aboard beside the government official who was just coming along for the ride. Overzealous, he offered to stay with us, should we need his help (what could he have done, exactly?), but his fear of the cold was obvious.

Seconds after liftoff, we were already clear of the mist and suspended in the blue. It was a perfect day for flying. I looked out the porthole as we flew over Customs.

"Right in there is our modem, Denis."

He looked at me and shrugged his shoulders. "We're in Nepal . . . "

We flew for about three quarters of an hour, catching only glimpses of our bearing through the portholes. The pilot, copilot, and flight engineer had a much better view from the cockpit. After a while, Denis and I looked at one another. We spoke at the same time.

"I think we're going too far east."

"I think we've already passed the Arun Valley."

While we were uttering these words, the engineer looked out of the cockpit and signaled for us to join him.

"The captain wants to know if you recognize our location, if this is the Arun Valley."

Denis and I stuck our heads inside the cockpit and started looking around, taking advantage of the improved view.

"Hey, Simone, we're going to the Kangchenjunga Valley," Denis exclaimed.

"Yes, that's right. We've gone way too far."

We told the pilot right away and asked him to change course, to double back. The captain carried out the maneuver, trusting to our directions.

After about five minutes, we sensed we were on the right course and yes, in fact, there was Tumlingtar, the only village in the area with an airport. So we started back up the Arun Valley. Once we reached Tashigaon, we got ready to land.

There was also a woman on board, the owner of the lodge where the porters had left our supplies. Like many other inhabitants of this region, she spent the winter in Kathmandu to avoid the extreme temperatures, since she could do so without losing business. I still don't know how Nima managed to find her in Kathmandu and offer to helicopter her back home. In theory, she should have been some help with guiding the pilot to a landing site, but in the end my memories from 1993 and Denis's more recent recollections from his winter attempt on Makalu the previous year proved more useful.

We set down in a wide clearing, a typical potato field. The locals were astonished. Our arrival would likely be the biggest news that week, maybe that whole month. The pilot cut the engine and gradually the rotor stopped turning. Once we were out of the helicopter, the first person we saw was Jagat. I hugged him and he proudly showed me all the gear stacked beside the pad, ready to be moved to base camp. The pilot and copilot came over and started calculating the weight of all our supplies.

"We should be able to get all of this to base camp in two trips. It's a bit below 5000 meters, right?"

"No, actually it's at 5600 meters. Hillary base camp is at 5000 but we need to go to advanced base camp, which is on the opposite face," I replied.

"Out of the question! We won't set down there. It's too high up and we've never been there. We go to the lower base camp."

Basically, I was getting this news a few minutes before liftoff. The pilots would be leaving us two days' walk from advanced base camp, below the south face instead of the west. But without porters, how would I get all the supplies and fuel for the stoves to the other side of the mountain?

I tried to convince the pilots, who politely but firmly said no. I quickly explained my problem to Jagat. He guaranteed me that, within a half hour, he'd find three or four porters willing to come along on the second flight and stay with us for the whole expedition. He made sure we had enough clothing and sleeping bags for them if needed but would also ask them to bring their own warm clothes (if they had them).

Once again, Jagat came through. We loaded half the gear onto the helicopter. Within a few minutes, the helicopter was flying north with Denis, the assistant cook Mingma, and a porter who, having caught scent of money, had gotten ready to leave in the blink of an eye.

Meanwhile, I was preparing the second load, and Jagat, quick as lightning, had already found two more local porters. In the span of ten minutes, they were ready to go.

The helicopter got back to Tashigaon in about half an hour. The pilots serviced it while we loaded the gear. We'd brought thirty 30-liter jerry cans of kerosene from Kathmandu. We were ready within ten minutes, and the Mi-17 set out again for the Hillary base camp at 4980 meters.

We landed without any trouble, unloaded everything, and a few seconds later the helicopter lifted off and disappeared from view. A surreal silence descended and with it the realization that we were finally at the base of "our" mountain with all of the necessary gear. We weren't on the face we'd chosen to climb, but that was a problem I felt capable of solving with the last-minute porters, who'd now become, in effect, essential members of our team.

It was already afternoon. We had just enough time to organize our stuff before it was time to take shelter. We used the only place available, a stone shack that served as a pantry in the spring and fall. Jagat had gotten the owner's permission to use it. We would keep a list of anything we used (jam, sugar, flour, candles, and not much else). For us it was mostly a defense against the freezing cold that hammered into us as soon as the sun went down.

The next day was cloudy and windy. Denis and I decided to acclimatize on the shoulder at the end of Makalu's long ridge, which was right above base camp. We got to 5300 meters. It was cold with strong winds, but I still tried the malfunctioning modem, hoping for miracles. It was no use.

On the second day, we'd planned to start moving gear to the other side of the mountain, carrying about thirty kilos per person. Unexpectedly, the weather was stupendous that day: sun, no wind, not a single cloud in the sky. On the fly, we changed our plans. I told Denis to fill the pack with climbing gear and whatever we'd need for three or four days. I don't know what put it in my head, but I wanted to try to reach at least 6000 meters via our chosen route on the other face. Oddly, Denis was of the same mind. We had no weather forecast to go by, just a hunch.

So we took our packs and set out. We walked along the moraine until we got past the labyrinth of stones and rock pillars covering the glacier. In the absence of any actual trail, it would have been easy to get lost. But once again we were able to draw on our experience with navigating this sort of terrain. Our route was long but surprisingly free of snow. We marked it with cairns to facilitate routefinding for Jagat, Mingma, and our porters, who were following behind us with their first loads.

We didn't make it to advanced base camp, though. We put up the tent at 5400 meters, about an hour away from our objective. The rest of our guys arrived later.

We didn't leave very early the next morning, given that we were waiting for the sun's warmth. And yes, even that morning, the weather was incredibly perfect for continuing our climb. At 5600 meters, we looked for a spot for our base camp or, even better, for the team to drop the gear so they could go back down for the next round.

We found a dip near some flat, convenient tent pads. People used these in spring and fall, but they were extremely exposed to the elements. Denis told me that the year before, his team had given in to the temptation to use these apparently ideal pads and had paid a steep price. Their tents had been partially destroyed by the wind, and they'd been left to battle the forces of nature without relief.

As a result, we declared the nearby uncomfortable but sheltered hollow I'd found as the ideal spot for base camp. It wasn't level, but we put our backs into filling it with a layer of rocks, using flat stones to create a sort of tiled, flat base. Just as we were finishing up, we found something odd: while arranging the stones, we uncovered human excrement. After swearing for a while, we deemed it an isolated incident . . . but soon we had all made the same "lucky" discovery. In short, we had just finished a mammothly huge job only to make camp on top of old latrines from summer expeditions.

Perhaps it would have been advisable to choose a different location. But faced with the thought of seven people having wasted an entire day at 5600 meters, we convinced ourselves that we could live with this "fragrant" mishap. We put up the mess tent, sealing the bottom of it as much as possible with heavy stones, and then stabilized it with ropes anchored to big rocks from the moraine.

Finally, the setup was done. In addition to the two sleeping tents for the Nepali staff, we put up two other small ones for Denis and me.

The night passed uneventfully. The next day the group split up. Jagat, Mingma, and the three porters headed down to 4980 meters for the rest of our gear. Denis and I went on climbing, aiming for 6100 meters and Camp 1.

The weather stayed stellar. A call to my meteorologist friend Karl Gabl pumped me up further. Three days of excellent weather with minimal winds was an ideal forecast for a summit bid, but having only acclimatized to 5555 meters at Chhukung Ri, an attempt seemed premature. We would certainly have risked both cerebral and pulmonary edema. On the other hand, in those unbelievable weather conditions it was unthinkable to limit ourselves to shuttling supplies between base camp and advanced base. We had five great Nepali porters for that. So Denis and I took advantage of the weather to further acclimatize and scout the route.

That day we moved particularly quickly. We reached 6100 meters in only three hours. We had all the supplies to establish Camp 1 at the border between the uppermost end of the moraine and the foot of the glacier, on the west face of Makalu. It was a fabulous, sun-kissed place, radiating heat thanks to its red rocks. We enjoyed this unexpected warmth for a couple of hours. Then, the second that ball of fire disappeared behind Baruntse, the Himalayan winter knifed us with its intense cold. A 30-degree drop in temperature within minutes: that's what happened whenever windless, sunny periods gave way to shade, or worse, when night fell.

Still, we were well equipped to spend the night at our highest altitude since the beginning of the expedition. We'd actually only slept at 4780 meters previously, at Ama Dablam View Lodge in Chhukung.

We were three days' climb away from Hillary base camp, where the helicopter had dropped us off.

We awoke to another gorgeous day, as Karl had predicted—our last. By normal standards of acclimatization, it would have been wise to descend. Being at 6100 meters only four days after leaving Kathmandu was a pretty big jump in altitude already.

But we wanted to use every opportunity to snatch meters on the mountain before the inevitable winter storm blew in. We didn't have headaches. This fact reassured us so we decided to go on climbing. We packed up all of our gear again, loaded our packs, and roped up. Then, with ice axes and crampons, we advanced onto the glacier. We followed a fairly linear course toward the change in grade at 6400 meters. A few crevasses blocked our way, but we always found an ice bridge over those deep, dark cracks. Being roped up was obligatory. Otherwise, a fall into any of those crevasses would have had fatal consequences.

The snow was hard, which enabled rapid progress. Our breathing quickened and our hearts beat faster. These were our bodies' strategies for coping with the drop in atmospheric pressure and thus in available oxygen as we gained altitude. We were in a state of acute hypoxia due to lack of acclimatization.

But we were determined to set up another camp, and maybe even sleep there. So we kept climbing.

A few clouds appeared in the sky, proof that the forecast had been bang-on. We got to the usual place for Camp 2 at 6750 meters. Despite the effort and altitude, we were doing well. So we decided to keep going to the higher Camp 2, a sort of terrace higher up. It was late afternoon when we took off our heavy packs and checked the altitude. The GPS read 6913 meters.

We began the hard work of digging and leveling a tent pad with our axes. It took about half an hour, but in the end we had a nearly perfect flat rectangle on which to pitch the tent. Within a few minutes, we were dashing inside. The cold was really biting, worsened by a light fog blocking the sun. After we'd organized our gear, we unrolled our sleeping mats and unstuffed our sleeping bags. Before we could sleep, though, we had to drink, and drink a lot, plus eat something. Hydration is essential for dealing with extreme altitudes, so you must drink to the point of nausea—one of my faults has always been a lack of discipline around hydration. We made some tea, and tortellini in soup, followed by a chunk of parmesan and a square of chocolate each, then off to beddy-bye.

We slept badly, me in particular. The effects of gaining 7000 meters in five days were coming home to roost. But I knew that bivying at that altitude would be important, a key stepping stone to succeeding in our winter ascent of Makalu.

The next morning, my eyes were quite swollen. Local edemas are a common sign of altitude's effects on those lacking acclimatization. I was nevertheless feeling reasonably good. We drank a little, ate a couple of packaged brioches, and then got ready for . . . more climbing! We aimed to exceed 7000 meters before going back to the lower camp. We wanted to recover some old fixed ropes. If we could locate them, they would be useful for our next ascent and descent. We got to 7050 meters in a couple of hours. I was dry heaving occasionally, but we were unwavering in our intention of making the most of every opportune moment.

The wind had picked up and the sky was clouding over, just as predicted, making the cold more brutal. We went back to the tent. We tried to speed everything up, to get down very quickly. At Camp 2, we took the tent down and dug a hole to bury our gear so it wouldn't be destroyed or blown away by the storm. Nothing remains unscathed in a 150-kilometer-per-hour wind. I was in the grip of dry heaves again but wasn't worried. I knew losing altitude would make me feel better.

I went back to helping Denis, and in a few minutes we had everything packed and buried. We used a couple of flags on bamboo sticks to mark the cache and started down, moving fast and following the other route markers we'd stuck in the snow the day before. About an hour later we were already at Camp 1, and we made it to advanced base camp in another hour.

The infamous mess tent, the one pitched on top of the summer's pit toilets, was the most beautiful and welcoming thing on the surface of the planet. Inside, the stoves gave off a slight warmth. The unpleasant odor didn't bother us much, partly because the altitude and the cold rendered it almost imperceptible and partly because we'd gotten used to it.

Jagat and Mingma congratulated us. Should they head down for a third load the next day, they wondered, or did we need them at advanced base camp?

"No, stay here tomorrow, Jagat. We need to set up the actual base camp. We have the big 2-meter dome tent to put up. We have to anchor it with a lot of rope, so it'll be secure."

"Okay. So we send the porters down alone?"

"Right. Tell them to make one last trip and then come up here to rest with us. I think we already have what we need for a couple of weeks, maybe three."

For dinner, we had spaghetti with tomato sauce and parmesan cheese straight from Italy. For our second course Jagat made roast chicken and, for dessert, fruit in syrup. Here, where the Nepalis slept alongside each other between the stoves and provisions, there was a significant difference in the internal and external temperature. The stoves warmed the kitchen tent (sacrificing scarce oxygen in the process, sadly). As a result, condensation had formed and frozen inside the kitchen, coating the entire surface of the tent in ice. Inside my warmest sleeping bag, I wore only long johns and a light turtleneck sweater. I crashed, partly from the built-up fatigue, partly from the soporific effect of sudden altitude changes.

I was awoken by Mingma's voice.

"Good morning, sir!"

It took me a few seconds to emerge from sleep and realize where I was.

"Good morning, Mingma . . . "

"Sir, I brought you some tea."

It's an indescribable feeling, being awoken like this at base camp on an 8000er after a long, deep sleep. Besides being a nearly over-the-top luxury, it's an act expressing simple and sincere affection.

"Thank you very much, Mingma."

The wind had picked up and from that day on, its sound was the background noise of our expedition. That constant, powerful rumble coming from Makalu's ridge was a clue to the force of the gusts at higher altitude. The clouds were traveling quickly, moving across the mountain with a fierce caress.

After a big breakfast, we all got to work. Putting up the big tent required time, precision, and a lot of attention to ensure that it was well anchored. We moved many heavy stones—while carefully avoiding the kitchen-slash-toilet area!

Periodically, a wind gust forced us to hold onto the tent with all our might, but eventually the dome tent was up, with virtually hurricane-proof anchoring. Once I'd identified the best place for our small one-kilowatt generator, I started to run cords out to the mess tent and dome tent for electricity.

The day was already coming to an end. We had just enough time to harvest some big blocks of ice from the glacier to melt for making supper and breakfast. The place was pretty dusty, but all in all it was pleasant and comfortable.

We'd planned to rest for two or three days before attempting a quick trip higher up, perhaps as far as the 7400-meter Makalu La. ("La" means "pass" in Tibetan.)

A call to Karl Gabl was in order.

"Ciao Karl, how's it going? Can you give me a weather report for the coming days?"

"For sure. Call me in an hour. I'll look at the mathematical models, cross-reference them with other data, and give you my interpretation. I'll have it for you in an hour."

I met Karl by chance in 2003. I was on Nanga Parbat, where he was forecasting for Gerlinde Kaltenbrunner and Robert Gasser's expedition. Robert was kind enough to share his contacts with me, and Karl and I have since become friends. I treat his weather reports almost as prophecy. I'm not exaggerating. Since 2003, he's never given me an incorrect forecast, so he has definitely earned and deserved my faith. These days, Karl manages to provide forecasts to some seventy expeditions annually—and he does it for free. He says it wouldn't be right to charge mountaineers when he's already paid by the Tyrolean weather service. This kind of person is practically extinct nowadays.

"Hello, Karl."

"Hi, Simone. I've looked into it and my forecast is . . . you'll need to be patient and stay in base camp. The weather conditions will definitely be adverse for any attempt to gain altitude. The winds will be powerful, temperatures will be arctic, especially above 7000 meters. So, take my advice. Relax and don't go up. You'd freeze and then get blown off the mountain."

"Okay, Karl. You've been very clear and persuasive."

"Sorry, but that's the forecast, Simone."

An authoritative phone call with an unequivocal message.

"Denis, we have to stay here. Karl says there'll be high winds, and coming from him that means there's really no hope."

"Right. Check out the ridge, Simone . . . the clouds are racing like a bullet train."

"So this means we'll rest and be ready for the next stage, going to Makalu La and spending the night."

A few days went by. We did some odd jobs, wrote on the computer, and chatted with our trusted Nepalis. They wanted to make another trip to Hillary base camp for kerosene and more food, taking advantage of the good weather before snow started to fall. The cold was our constant companion, made even more stinging by high-altitude winds that drove temperatures in the camp to below –20 degrees Celsius at night.

On our fourth rest day, we decided to have a puja, a Buddhist purification ceremony invoking the Buddha's protection. This ceremony is fundamental to any expedition in Nepal or Tibet. According to Buddhist belief, the Divine dwells on the planet's highest mountain peaks. You must be purified before venturing into that realm, in order to come back alive. Usually, a lama from the nearest monastery is called upon to preside over the ceremony, but in some cases the task is carried out by the eldest Sherpa or the most charismatic Nepali.

Jagat was therefore the most appropriate person to conduct the ceremony. We built an altar, a perfect cube made of stones and carefully positioned on a raised area. We then placed a large wooden pole into the middle of it. Another expedition had left the pole there after using it for the same purpose. We tied long cables to the top of the pole and extended them out to each of the four cardinal points, so that the request for purification and protection would spread everywhere. Along the cables we hung cloth flags in the colors of the five elements, on which prayers were written. The flapping of these flags would release an infinite, constant stream of prayers into the air around Makalu.

The ceremony lasted no more than half an hour. Despite the sunshine, we were feeling the wind and cold so Jagat tried to speed things up. Our gear was also blessed at the foot of the small rudimentary altar, after which the ceremony concluded with the tossing of rice and flour into the air, accompanied by cries of joy from all and sundry.

The climbing gear went back inside our tent, naturally, but the flags, rice, and flour stayed on the altar, where the crows and the wind would take care of them during the course of the expedition.

I stayed in my tent listening to music for about an hour, after which Mingma came to call me for lunch. Jagat had put together an excellent banquet of pasta al pesto, meat, and polenta. Each had to be wolfed down quickly, before the cold snatched all their heat away.

Near the end of our meal, we heard a whistle. Strange. There was no one outside. Everyone was inside the tent. We waited a moment and kept our ears cocked. Another whistle, followed by a shout.

We rushed outside and saw a Nepali porter nimbly carrying a moderately sized load. He was walking toward us.

"Well, look at that! It's my uncle," said Mingma, running to meet him.

The two hugged and headed over to us.

"The modem has arrived, sir!"

Denis and I both let out a hoot of joy at the same time. We thanked the porter and, after giving him a megatip, invited him to join us at the table.

I used a knife to slit open this precious cargo and found a letter from my friends at Intermatica: "Hi, Simone. Hope this modem has arrived to the right destination in time. We tested it and it works perfectly. Sorry for the other one. It was a preview model sent to us by the head office. Insert the SIM card from the malfunctioning modem and follow the pointing and line acquisition procedures. Call if you have problems. Good luck! Ruggero and team."

I picked up the new Thuraya modem, unscrewed the protective cover, inserted the SIM card from the broken modem, and followed the instructions to the letter.

"Thuraya . . . pointing . . . signal at 74 percent (good) . . . acquiring . . . standard!"

I was connected, finally able to send photos and film clips of our story, of the adventure we were on. No one has ever obliged me to share like this or has provided incentives. It's my choice. I like sharing my emotions "live" with whoever wishes to listen. The account I gave that day was longer than usual, with photos of our camp and surrounding landscape. When that was finished, I called Ruggero, Simona, and Fabrizio in Rome and thanked them for the modem.

After that break, we decided to head out again and try climbing higher than the time before. Forty-eight hours of mild weather was all we would need. We didn't even call Karl for a report. We trusted our intuition. Besides, even if we were wrong, nothing bad would come of it.

We maintained a good rhythm and were at Camp 2 by midday. We were dressed lightly, perhaps too lightly. We dug up the gear we'd buried and set up camp. That night was particularly harsh. I recall being numb with cold despite being fully clothed inside my sleeping bag.

The next day we left without packs, heading directly for Makalu La. At 7100 meters we found the first of the fixed ropes. The rope was partly hidden in the snow and iced over. Digging it out with our axes was slow, heavy work that winded us and sucked all the energy out of our arms. We managed to free meter after meter of rope, quite a good length of it. But on many other sections, we had to climb on belay.

The wind gusts were truly horrible, so bad that they actually managed to physically move us at times, and just as we were climbing the steepest section of the couloir, too. We weren't able to film ourselves anymore.

We just snapped a few photos and then continued on with the big job of digging out the fixed rope for another hour.

We came to a section of rock where a black fixed rope hung down from above. We couldn't tell if it was still well anchored and in good condition or worn out and therefore too dangerous to use. We decided not to risk it and climbed without the help of that long black line. Those 15 meters of rock proved quite challenging, made more so by a very short overhanging section. We climbed above it and noticed that the rope disappeared into the snow. Was it was securely anchored under there or just a length of loose rope? Who knows.

We reached 7300 meters. Because we were quite high up already, we sensed that the end of the couloir was not much farther. We were exhausted but the main thing was the wind, lashing us more and more fiercely as we went on. We clapped our hands together a lot to stimulate circulation and avoid frostbite. We couldn't make out any old rope above us. This meant simul-climbing.

The thought of our descent was more worrisome still. There was little snow in this part of the couloir—it was all hard ice. A slip would be disastrous.

We decided to descend. We'd done an excellent job. We'd reached 7300 meters and salvaged some sections of rope in the couloir. It had been an important step in our acclimatization, too, so there was a lot to be pleased about.

To avoid using up the fuel and food at our last camp, which was only 400 meters away, we decided to go back to base camp. Jagat and Mingma were down there, 1600 meters below us, and we were resolutely determined to join them before nightfall. We descended quickly and decisively. Available oxygen increases as you lose altitude, producing an energizing effect—our pace quickened. Within a few hours, we were once again safe at advanced base camp.

We spent four days resting at 5600 meters with the Nepali team. The wind had come back with a vengeance. Its background noise was getting more noticeable, whether it was day or night. *Woooom, woooom* . . . a haunting rumble that instilled dread. We could only hope it wouldn't change direction and blow through our camp with that same force. It would have destroyed everything. Many times on those nights we left our tents to further reinforce them. Some gusts had moved large stones and sheared away a stabilizing rope. The sheer force was truly scary and the word "hurricane," which Karl had used in his forecasts, was definitely fitting.

After spending yet another night battered by the wind, I called him.

"Hi, Karl. The wind tossed us around again last night. There's no sign of it letting up."

"I have some news for you."

"Really? Tell me!"

"I see a three-day window of pretty good weather, but with increasing wind. Tomorrow it'll be 40 kilometers per hour; the day after, 70; the third day, 90. Then the jet stream will come through again, the hurricane, whatever you want to call it."

"Wow, great, thanks Karl!"

"Simone, wait. Promise me you'll go back to base camp in three days' time. Promise me that. Listen, if you stay up on the mountain in that wind, you'll die." Karl's warning was serious, almost strict.

"Okay, Karl. I promise. I'll still call you every day, even from the higher camps, so you can confirm the weather and update me on any developments."

"Sounds good, Simone, ciao and good luck. Say hi to Denis for me."

I relayed the latest weather report to Denis, and we immediately decided to leave the next day. We aimed to reach Makalu La and establish a camp for the night. It would be the highest point on Makalu ever reached in winter, in twenty-nine years.

We prepared our gear and packed some extra food, a gas cartridge, a change of personal clothing, and our high-altitude suits. I also packed my American sponsor's ultralight two-person tent. Just off the assembly line, it weighed 1.5 kilos in total. The idea was to use it once we'd gotten beyond our highest previous bivy at 6900 meters.

We left around 10:30 a.m. Jagat burned incense in a cleft of the altar we'd used for the puja. He said good-bye to us first; then Mingma and the other Nepali porters bid us well. We exchanged good-byes and left at a brisk pace. We wanted to make the most of those seventy-two hours of "human" weather before the storm hit.

We were extremely fast, faster than we expected. We reached 6900 meters in less than four hours. We dug out all of the equipment and set up camp.

The first day of climbing had gone well. We weren't even that tired, so the vibe was quite good. We ate tortellini with parmesan, followed by salami, cheese, and crackers. We shared a small potful of tea and lay down in our sleeping bags. The night passed pretty well, even though we were startled awake numerous times by the tent fabric snapping suddenly with the wind gusts.

We left at 7:25 the next morning. It's always hard to leave any earlier than that in wintertime because the cold is so intense. Often your hands and feet freeze before you even get moving.

Despite the 70-kilometer-per-hour winds Karl had forecast, we still aimed to climb to Makalu La and spend the night, descending to base camp on the third and last day of favorable weather—the one forecast for 90-kilometer-per-hour winds. Sleeping at 7400 meters would also be very important for maximizing our acclimatization. The previous night had been only our second one at 6900 meters since the start of the expedition. Because Makalu is 8500 meters, it requires perfect acclimatization—500 meters might not seem like much, but they make a huge difference once you're above 8000 meters.

We set out with resolve, wearing our high-altitude suits, balaclavas, down mittens, and thick merino wool socks inside our mountaineering boots. After about an hour of climbing, we found the first of the rope we'd extracted from the snow and ice. That helped us along for the next hundred or so meters, and then we continued without it, tied in to each other along our dynamic safety rope. We continued on, simul-climbing, careful not to make any mistakes. The danger of a potentially fatal slip increased as the couloir grew progressively steeper.

We reached the section of vertical rock. We'd rigged it with a length of 5-millimeter rope on our previous visit. Given the rope's minimal thickness, we preferred to free climb and clip in to it only for added safety. We got past that section quite nimbly and kept climbing. Since we hadn't gone beyond that point before, we were now traveling through unknown territory. With every meter, we found ourselves more exposed to the whirlwind. Plunging into the couloir, the wind created vortices strong enough to lift us off our feet. We kept our ice axes anchored as best we could and proceeded with maximum caution. After about an hour of laborious progress in the shade, the last part of the couloir appeared, lit up by the sun. The last stretch was hard ice. We stuck to the left as much as possible, staying near the rock so we could advance on slightly more favorable ground.

We came across a hanging rope, whipping in the wind. We clipped an ascender on but didn't put our weight on it. The protection was psychological more than anything. The hard-packed snow of the final meters was perfect for crampons, which also relieved the tension somewhat.

When we finally made it to Makalu La, there was plenty of wind but, thankfully, also a lot of sunshine. The rays warmed our bones a bit and shored up our courage. But it was still early. The big saddle of Makalu's pass was an icy sheet. A few old, shredded tents abandoned by previous expeditions fluttered from their anchors in the ice.

"How's it going, Simone?"

"Good, Denis. You?"

"I'm good, too. We're at 7400 meters. Good job!"

"Thanks. You've done well, too. Listen, we have a few more hours of light, and the wind seems bearable. Why don't we keep climbing a bit instead of stopping here?"

"Good idea, I'm in. Let's go!"

And so our break at Makalu La lasted only a few minutes, just long enough to consult with one another before continuing.

We climbed to 7700 meters despite the wind, cold, and effects of altitude. We set up our ultralight tent there.

Denis hopped inside to keep it from flying off, while I filled the tent's stuff sack with ice. Our actions were extremely fast and efficient. Denis even managed to film this frenzied activity. Very soon, I was inside the tent shaking hands with Denis. It was the highest point anyone had ever reached on Makalu during the winter, and we were pleased. It was something of a success, but a partial one. We were there to make a summit bid and now we had only twenty-four hours to rest and get down before the "hurricane" arrived.

Once the stove was on, I took my boots off. My feet were cold so I started to massage them, careful not to crowd the flame. The lack of oxygen affected not only our lungs but also the stove's feeble flame, which seemed as tired as we were.

We got into our sleeping bags right away and stayed there while we cooked, chatted, and took pictures. It was the only way we could stay warm. While we ate, we planned the day ahead, the one forecasted for winds of 90 kilometers per hour.

"Listen, Denis. What if we climbed a little more tomorrow, before heading down?"

"You read my mind. All things considered, we're doing well despite the altitude. If we wake up without any particular problems and if the weather conditions are stable, we can try it."

"What time should we get up?"

"Four. We'll get ready, drink something, and go."

"Okay, I'm with you. We'd better sleep now."

We didn't rest much, worrying constantly about the coming twenty-four hours. It's possible that neither of us had completely revealed our intentions . . .

We awoke at the appointed time. The tent's interior was completely iced up. It was insanely cold, below –40 degrees Celsius. We'd slept in our high-altitude suits and boot liners to stay as warm as possible.

The morning's procedures were fast, as befitted the situation. We'd no sooner unzipped the tent than the wind gusted a flurry of snow inside. It wound up everywhere—in the sleeping bags, on the sleeping mats, in the little pot we'd just used.

We put on our crampons, decided to save weight by not bringing the pack, and set off. Knowing there were crevasses, we roped up. Our first steps took forever. The cold took our breath away. Warming our frozen muscles took a tremendous effort but we eventually got into a rhythm: twenty or twenty-five steps followed by a rest to catch our breath. We repeated this sequence over and over again, like robots. We wore ski goggles to protect our eyes. I was wearing a neoprene face mask as well, while Denis kept his face buried in the collar of his heavy jacket.

The gusts were indeed tremendous, impossible to overcome. When we felt them coming, we could do little but crouch, clip in to the ice axes, and wait. The first few hours of that morning were primarily a struggle against fatigue and wind. We looked at each other, occasionally gestured to one another, but neither of us so much as hinted at the idea of going down. We just kept climbing.

We worked around a large serac, climbed straight upward alongside it, and then traversed to the left toward some rocks. There, we stopped.

"How's it going, Simone?"

"Good, I'm good. It's fucking cold and this wind is hell, but I'm good, I'm still strong."

"Perfect. Me too. We're at 8000 meters and it's only midmorning. We're doing well."

"Yes, yes we are. Now we climb this section of rock to get to the ridge, right?"

"Exactly. Come on, Simone, let's go."

We hadn't said it openly yet, but those words left no doubt as to our intentions. We were going for the summit, contrary to the forecast and expectations. We followed only instinct and our shared ambition.

Getting through the wind-exposed couloir that led to the east ridge of Makalu was particularly tricky. We used the classic lead-climbing method of alternating belays. It was a huge fight to not be torn off the mountain by the wind. We progressed in fits and starts, moving only when the gusts abated.

In another hour and a half, we were on the ridge at 8200 meters. From there we could see a rocky shoulder, beyond which we were supposed to be able to see the summit. The snow was hard on the ridge but there were rock pinnacles to be bypassed.

We reached the base of the buttress, the shoulder that blocked our view of the summit. The snow was strangely fresh there, sugary, and with every step upward we slid relentlessly back down. Playing the edge between snow and rock, we managed to proceed. Near the summit we glimpsed an old piece of rope half buried in the fresh snow. I pulled it out with one hand while holding my ice ax in place with the other. The rope was no longer useful for climbing but would come in handy on the descent.

We continued climbing the last dangerous meters of that buttress until we were able to skirt it on the left and get back onto the ridge.

The summit was there in front of us, so close yet so far away. We were at around 8400 meters with another 80-ish meters to climb, followed by an exposed knife-edged ridge. The wind gusts had become a permanent feature intensifying the cold. We made our way cautiously along that blade of snow—it was very sharp, as though the ridge were protecting the summit from being conquered. We moved one at a time, belaying each other. Denis set off, carefully, while I fed him tiny bits of slack. I was anchored to an old piton. It had been used by previous expeditions but was still holding fast. It would certainly have arrested a fall.

Thanks to the good consistency of the snow, Denis was able to pick up his pace. He was a couple of meters below the ridgeline, which enabled him to make an agile traverse to within 20 meters of the summit. He stopped, signaled for me to catch up to him, and gave me the thumbs-up. That was a good sign, without a doubt. I followed his footsteps and climbed up to where he'd stopped. There was a length of fixed rope leading to within 5 meters of the summit. He asked if he could traverse first, knowing the way was secure and less challenging than the previous stretch.

"Okay, Denis, go for it!"

This last, fairly easy traverse was the highest, most exposed, and most beautiful of the climb. Denis stopped again and signaled for me to climb on. The rhythm was now ten steps followed by thirty seconds to catch our breath, and so on. We gulped air with our mouths wide open, starved for oxygen. Every –50-degree mouthful was a knife to the lungs, an agony necessary for survival.

I joined Denis 5 meters below the summit.

"You go first, Simone. You deserve it. I'll belay you from here. Then come down and I'll go up."

"No, Denis. Let's go together!"

"Simone, that's not a good idea. You see how this snow tower is super sharp at the top? You go. I'll film you and then you film and photograph me."

"Okay, Den, I'll go."

Those steps I took at 1:30 p.m. on February 9, 2009, were the longest, hardest, and most joyous of my life. I decided to climb right up to the final centimeter of the peak and lean my hips against the highest possible point of Makalu. On the summit, I was oxygen deprived—I fell to my knees, but not out of emotion. I rested my head on the snow in an attempt to snatch some precious molecules of oxygen from the ice-cold air. After a few seconds, I turned toward Denis, lifted my arms, and shouted my triumph with whatever air I'd managed to get into my lungs.

As soon as I dropped my arms, I swung and sank my ice ax into the snowcapped summit. I channeled everything into that motion, all my effort, joy, energy, rage. I couldn't have prevented myself from taking that swing even if I'd tried. That swing was for all the people over the years who'd done nothing but hassle me about why I share, why I talk, why I write, why I climb, why I fly, why, why, why . . .

Controversy has always been part of mountaineering and up there, at 8500 meters, I should have ignored the buzz of all that chatter. But I couldn't. I am not a machine. I wanted to show that. And I wanted people to see that the tiny pebble I'd repeatedly put into my own shoe had transformed into a boulder now capable of crushing all those petty lovers of controversy.

My anger quickly dissolved, though. It gave way to an exultation so overflowing and so strong as to be forever ingrained in my memory. It's difficult to describe the emotions of such a moment. It's like trying to describe love, the elation and positivity you experience when you completely surrender to it.

My brother Denis Urubko was there, my close friend since Annapurna, and that made the moment even better. Twelve years had passed since the tragedy in 1997 and now, at last, there was a Kazakhstani beside me on the summit of an 8000er in winter—and what an 8000er it was!

I stayed just a few minutes and then descended to make room for Denis on the summit. The wind was strong enough to create a whirlwind of snow around us, and the ice crystals sliced at our faces.

When I got to Denis, I hugged him and said, "It's your turn. Go on, I'll take pictures of you and film it. Then we have to think about going back down. Don't forget what Karl said. If he knew we were up here . . . "

Denis summited. He, too, lifted his arms in victory and smiled. I had just enough time to snap a few pictures before he came back down.

"Okay, Simone, let's get down. You first."

After that outcome, everything seemed easier. It was our last day of reasonably adequate weather. The storm was on its way, which may have been what spurred us on—we descended surprisingly quickly and confidently.

Only after getting around and past the serac did I feel the fatigue take hold of my legs. I often had to sit down in the snow. Although even Denis had slowed noticeably, we were still quite calm, and quite close to our last tent at 7700 meters.

We reached it by evening, in the dregs of daylight.

We wearily got inside, looked at each other and smiled. We took off our mitts and shook hands enthusiastically.

"Now what, Denis? I think it would be better to sleep here and go down to advanced base camp tomorrow without any breaks. The weather will be awful but we'll be less exposed to the wind as we go down, you'll see."

"Okay, yeah, I agree. We need to drink and eat something and it's already dark. We have to have the light and enough energy to get down the couloir to Makalu La."

The night flew by. We alternated between sleep and wakefulness, during which we reflected on the day's achievements. Our satisfaction was muted by knowing we were still very high up on the mountain.

The tent was well anchored to the ice, but it flapped continually in the wind and even flattened on top of us. Karl had been right. The wind was definitely getting stronger and gusting more frequently.

We set out at first light. Pushed along by the wind, we descended quickly to Makalu La. The sun was rising but its rays weren't yet reaching us. We approached the steep, icy couloir that led down to Camp 2. Using some stretches of rope and facing into the mountain while downclimbing, we lost more altitude. Once in the couloir, the wind became a whirlwind. There was no way to protect ourselves from it. It blew from every direction and got inside everything. We withstood it and continued our progress. We were almost obsessed by a single basic need: get down, get down, get down.

We got to the vertical rock pitch and lowered ourselves on the thin Dyneema rope we'd fixed previously. We knew the rope was very strong and the anchor was solid. Even so, trusting your life to a mere 5 millimeters of nylon makes quite the impression on a person.

We were in the couloir once again but the grade was easing, allowing us to climb facing outward for longer stretches until it became the only way to proceed.

Finally, we glimpsed our little Camp 2 tent at 6900 meters. The yellow fabric showed us the way through the blizzard and we reached it in the blink of an eye. We packed everything up as quickly as possible. Even though it made our packs extremely heavy, we filled them absurdly full. We couldn't relax just yet. We rested not even a minute before setting out again. Knowing there were crevasses everywhere, we roped up. We couldn't afford to make any mistakes.

Thanks to the lower altitude, the wind was abating and the surrounding ridges sheltered us from its fury. We started to look forward to some safety, and our descent became more relaxed. The packs, however, were destroying our shoulders, and back pain had set in. We were at 6400 meters by now, on a wide, safe plateau. The sun was even shining and the wind wasn't bothering us much. Nevertheless, we remained roped together and silent, thinking only of getting down, putting one foot in front of the other.

At 6200 meters, we found a surprise. Jagat and Mingma were climbing toward us without crampons, just mountaineering boots. We'd given them news of our success from Makalu La. They'd decided to come up and meet us with tea and cookies.

We were filled with joy at the sight of them. The meeting with our two angels from base camp was incredibly fraternal, with big hugs, pats on the back, and more hugs. Denis and I sucked back two cups of sweet tea each and ate a few cookies. Then we all headed back toward base camp together. It came into sight around 2:00 in the afternoon. Our base camp may have been sitting on top of old summertime latrines, but that day it was the most beautiful and sweet-smelling encampment in all the Himalaya.

Once there, Jagat dashed into the mess tent to light stoves and prepare food. Denis and I reached toward each other and shook hands firmly, then we drew each other in for one last liberating hug.

The last Nepalese 8000er in the Himalaya had been summited in winter. You could even say it was the last page in the story of first winter ascents in that part of the mountain range. Twenty-nine years had passed since the first winter attempt on Makalu and as many years from the very first winter ascent of an 8000er, on Everest. Polish climbers Wielicki and Cichy had officially started the Himalayan story that February 17, 1980. Denis and I had ended it nearly thirty years later in our light-and-fast style of climbing. Ours was a different approach to mountaineering that had evolved precisely because of those who had preceded us. The Makalu expedition had taken us only nineteen days from arrival at base camp. We had summited, not with a team, but as a pair of climbers. And we'd done it without using oxygen or high-altitude Sherpas, and without preparing the face in advance.

Makalu was Denis's second winter ascent with me and our first 8000er together. For me, it was my second big dream come true, another unforgettable ascent made possible by a combination of ability, determination, good luck, and willpower.

I had suffered frostbite to my feet. I sent pictures of my purple toes to a trusted doctor in Italy. He absolutely prohibited me from walking in the coming days, as this could cause infection with potentially grave consequences, up to and including amputation.

Not being in a position to tackle the remaining days of trekking that Makalu entailed, I called Nima in Kathmandu. He did his best and found a helicopter. However, it could only touch down where this had all begun—Hillary base camp, 700 meters below us.

After taking the tents down, I gave our Nepali team precise instructions on carrying the gear down and organizing a new caravan of porters. I hugged and thanked each of them individually, adding a generous tip. I left my satellite phone with Jagat so we could stay in contact.

Then Denis and I started valleyward on foot. Since the helicopter had already been scheduled for the next day, we aimed to get down before nightfall. The long walk caused some pain in my toes, but it was tolerable. We chatted happily for hours, my friend and I. Only then did we start to relax and savor some satisfaction from our climb. Our thoughts had already turned to the future, to home, a hot shower, and spring.

It was almost dark when we arrived at Hillary base camp. In the shelter, within four walls and with a roof over our heads, we felt safe. We slept deeply indeed, aided by the soporific effect of the now oxygen-rich air.

The next morning we rose early. At 7:00, we heard the helicopter in the distance. We left the shelter as it approached, banking near the south face of Makalu before nosing into the wind and coming in for a landing. It touched down rather gently. The door opened and the pilot signaled for us to board. Denis took a seat in the back along with our packs. They were light, containing only our most important and valuable things. I sat up front in the copilot seat.

The helicopter was an Ecureuil 350 B, the oldest and least powerful model and also the only one available that morning, as the others were already booked. The pilot's name was something else: Sherchan Ashish.

Once the doors were closed, Ashish prepared for liftoff. He raised us only half a meter off the ground, letting the helicopter ride on the updraft and skim the ground as he picked up speed. We were up to speed and he was about to gain altitude when suddenly we heard a crack. One of the skids had hit a rock—fortunately without consequence for either helicopter or passengers, so we finally became airborne.

During that very beautiful hour-and-a-half flight to Kathmandu, we talked over the headsets. We befriended the pilot, but who could have guessed that I would be Ashish's colleague two years later? That I would be a pilot as well, working for the same company in which he was a partner? In fact, Fishtail Air has become like a family to me. It provides the ideal framework for carrying out my project of creating a (heretofore nonexistent) helicopter rescue unit in the Himalaya.

Not long after the Makalu climb, I decided to go to California to get my pilot's license for both private and commercial helicopters, as well as my type rating for three kinds of aircraft, two of which were specifically meant for flying in the mountains. Meanwhile, a friend back in Italy, Gianni Carminati, offered to sponsor my training by letting me fly his personal helicopter free of charge, the kind most suitable for high-altitude flying. So I gained experience, built a team, and was able to kick-start this other life alongside mountaineering. I attended the Civil Aviation Academy in Kathmandu. For two seasons now, I have been alternating between mountaineering and being a rescue pilot in Nepal with Fishtail Air.

WE'VE ARRIVED AT CAMP 2. It was a hard climb but we're feeling good. We just finished setting up the tent on a ledge. Now we're burrowed in, warming ourselves and resting up in preparation for tomorrow's hard work. Camp 3 awaits.

We left Camp 2 at eight in the morning. At two, we pitched the tent at Camp 3 (6600 meters). It's very cold—the radio is iced up and the batteries are dead. The weather is still satisfactory, so tomorrow we plan to climb some more. Our idea is to get to 7100 meters, even higher if we can. Then we'll go back to base camp to regain our strength.

CHAPTER 8

MISSION NEAR-IMPOSSIBLE

(GASHERBRUM II)

AT THE END OF 2009, I decided to pause a moment and consider what my winter ascents of Shishapangma and Makalu had sparked. Undeniably, they had given new life to a trend, to a way of experiencing and exploring mountains that's nearly always neglected: the way of winter mountaineering. Since 2005, at least four or five teams have undertaken this type of expedition each year. In addition to this being a great thing for mountaineering in general, it gives me pride to have revived the style first created by the Polish in the 1980s.

I hadn't enjoyed a winter at home in seven years. It was wonderful. What's more, my wife, Barbara Zwerger, gave birth to Jonas that same winter. My daughter from a previous relationship, born in 1999, joyfully welcomed her little brother.

For a mountaineer who's nomadic at least half of the year and busy with one expedition or another, maintaining a stable, long-term relationship and having a family is not easy. And I mean "having a family" in the fullest, most actively involved and enlightened sense. But with Barbara, a competitive ice climber at the World Cup level, I seem to have struck a balance—still, tremendous effort is required because I'm not at home much; even when I'm not on an expedition, I'm out and about networking and the like.

Barbara adapted to my nomadic lifestyle quickly. She has accompanied me to some of the most isolated parts of the world and been part of some expeditions. Even now with Jonas in the picture, she still manages to sustain and support (or put up with!) me in this seemingly crazy life, calmly carrying on with our relationship and our family.

Naturally, my vacation couldn't last all of 2010. I accepted the job of guiding a friend, Aldo (a sporty, mountain-loving notary), up Everest. With a decade of experience and a few serious expeditions under his belt, he was no amateur.

Having brilliantly completed the process of acclimatization, Aldo unfortunately developed stomach problems at a crucial juncture of the expedition. I had him evacuated from base camp by helicopter and on a plane immediately back to Italy, where he was diagnosed with a fairly serious form of food-borne illness.

As a result, I found myself alone at base camp. I decided to climb Everest anyway, since the permit was paid and everything was ready. It was my fourth time standing on the planet's highest point. Climbing-wise, I wasn't very satisfied because I had started using supplemental oxygen at 8500 meters to avoid frostbite on my feet. I could have turned back, it's true, rather than climb in other than my preferred style. But it was an amazing day and I preferred to enjoy the exciting if typical climb to the summit, surrounded by an unforgettable view.

While I'd been at home in the winter of 2009–10, several expeditions had taken place in Pakistan. Two different teams had tried for Nanga Parbat and Broad Peak. After a nearly head-to-head struggle lasting two months, both had given up. This was understandable. I know how harsh the winter can be in the Karakoram, and on Nanga Parbat too (which is actually in the Himalaya). I myself had failed twice, even though the second time I'd been been a mere step away from success.

Soon after these attempts, I read an ExplorersWeb interview with Polish climber Artur Hajzer and came across something that stopped me in my tracks and sparked the idea that became a sort of obsession: "Maybe it really is impossible to climb an 8000-meter peak in the Karakoram in winter."

This from the famous spokesperson of his country's golden era of alpinism, a man who led the Polish expedition to Broad Peak, a man with the first winter ascent of Annapurna under his belt!

It was like a bucket of ice water in the face, a kick in the pants, but above all it was a source of inspiration. "What's that you say? Impossible? No way. Don't ever use that word in life, especially not in mountaineering!"

Hajzer's thought, uttered in the heat of the moment—likely something he let slip after a long, losing battle—became the fuse that reignited my enthusiasm.

"Okay, fine," I said to myself. "Next winter I'll go to Broad Peak, and then we'll see what's impossible. I've gotten to within 200 meters of the summit. I'm convinced there's nothing impossible about it!"

And so I started mentally preparing myself for my third expedition to Broad Peak. I had no doubt as to the first member of my expedition team. It would be Denis Urubko. Tackling Broad Peak as a duo would be more than sufficient. We'd done it that way on Makalu as well. I started to get used to the idea.

But then another bit of news shuffled the cards. My friend Artur Hajzer was to make another attempt on Broad Peak. What to do? I could hardly claim priority access. There were only two options: find myself on the same mountain as another expedition, making the same attempt for a historic first; or choose another objective and avoid a dangerous "race."

While I was considering these alternatives, three other winter expeditions in Pakistan were announced: an international one guided by Austrian Gerfried Goetschl on Gasherbrum I and two on Nanga Parbat, one Polish and the other a solo Russian.

This development, this renewed interest in winter ascents of 8000ers, was good to see . . . but what was I to do now?

The only two "free" mountains were the infamous K2 and the smaller, yet still dangerous Gasherbrum II. Why did I choose the latter? Well, G does come before K, alphabetically speaking . . . All jokes aside, I made my decision based on logic after analyzing the level of difficulty and the probability of success. The fact that a first winter ascent in Pakistan had been sought in vain since 1987 meant it was a truly arduous endeavor. There was no need to start with the most difficult summit first, especially given that ours would be a light expedition without any high-altitude porters or supplemental oxygen.

My ongoing second thoughts were not only about the goal. By the time I finally chose Gasherbrum II, I had also changed my mind about the team. I wanted to add another element, an alpinist who was also skilled with photography and video and could capture the realities of winter in Pakistan and of an expedition in that season.

When I asked the American Cory Richards to join Denis and me, I was following my intuition. I had a hunch. We were all on The North Face team, but besides that the three of us were from different continents and had different histories and personalities. An American, a Kazakhstani, and an Italian: it sounds like the start of an old joke, but it turned out to be the beginning of an exciting tale of a lifetime.

When I made my choice of Cory public on my website, I initially received messages, emails, and comments from people either wanting explanations or warning me, people who believed it was an error to invite someone who'd climbed only one 8000er (Lhotse) and, moreover, had used oxygen. Hardly anyone was aware that Cory had successfully done two winter expeditions in Nepal, both challenging, on two different 6000ers via new routes. His use of oxygen on Lhotse had been inevitable because he'd done the climb after ten days in base camp near the end of the season. Cory also had a great desire to learn, wasn't arrogant in the least, and was an excellent photographer into the bargain.

In short, I decided once again to gamble on my intuition. Denis trusted me. He assured me that he agreed without a doubt with the reasons for my choice. Nevertheless, I knew Cory would have to face a difficult task from the outset—earning Denis's trust. Denis doesn't trust easily. He's skeptical, always on the defensive. Not a signal, movement, or word gets past him. Plus, he suffers from a kind of "Soviet syndrome": he can't hug or kiss Americans. So I was going to have quite the job to do, but I knew we had the right ingredients for a solid, harmonious team.

We arrived in Islamabad a couple of days after Christmas (respecting December 21, as always, for me an iron-clad rule). After the usual meeting with the Pakistan Alpine Club and the sorting of supplies shipped from Italy, we finally boarded a flight for Skardu on January 3, 2011. We flew very close to Nanga Parbat's Diamir Face. All three of us were glued to the little window, taking pictures and filming. Cory, superprofessional from the get-go, used his small tripod and reflex cameras.

It was a spectacular flight, and even coming in for a landing at Skardu was smooth and stunning. The plane practically has to nosedive from 7000 meters to the airport at 2000, banking three times within the Indus Valley. Upon landing, foreigners are asked to fill in a form.

There are six or seven intelligence agencies in Pakistan that "dissect" and surveil all visitors, especially those heading into the northern part of the country. Even in the hotels, someone shows up every so often requesting information about the guests. If you're not aware of this, you might not notice it. But after my many years of traveling in Pakistan, certain details no longer escape me.

We planned to acclimatize on Kosar Gang, a 6400-meter peak two hours from Skardu by jeep. Base camp is three hours' walk from the road.

Upon landing the next day, we took a jeep in the direction of Askole. A couple of hours later, we stopped near a group of houses where a small crowd of men and children awaited us. They were our porters and their sons, who'd come to see them off. We unloaded all the gear and supplies for a week of acclimatizing on the mountain that rose 4400 meters above us.

While the porters divided the loads, we were hosted in an unfurnished but welcoming room where we were offered tea and biscuits. About half an hour later, we started up the mountain. The day was calm and cold but pleasant due to the sunshine. For the first hour we climbed together single file. Once the loads began to weigh more heavily, naturally the porters began to take breaks. Cory and I continued on at a brisk pace while Denis took it a bit easier, stopping now and again to take some pictures.

In less than three and a half hours we reached base camp at 3700 meters. It was a shack that didn't seem any more hospitable than the stone goat enclosure beside it.

After Denis, the porters gradually began to arrive: Didar, the cook; his assistant, Saeed Jan; and Hassan, a kind of sirdar and base-camp manager with a long alpine career and two 8000ers to his credit.

We set up our tents in the enclosure, on top of frozen dung. Our Pakistani staff quickly installed the mess tent and got busy preparing tea and a hot meal. Once they were unburdened, we paid the porters who were then free to quickly head for the valley. That spot was really beautiful. It had an incredible view, and the peace was surreal.

Strangely enough, the expedition period is the only relaxed part of my year, a stress- and problem-free time. With the exception of the place I'm currently writing from, expeditions are my only break from regular life. No doubt it's my own fault that my life is so jam-packed with commitments and projects. While on an expedition, I have the luxury and privilege of not needing to constantly check a watch or a daily agenda. My only concerns are whether or not to climb and ensuring the logistics are working—nothing more.

I remember my time in Kosar Gang base camp as being the first time in months that my mind was clear. All that lay ahead of me was acclimatization and preparation for the project close to my heart: proving whether a winter ascent of an 8000er in the Karakoram and in Pakistan really was impossible.

The next day, after climbing up a long snow slope that must have been grassy during the summer, we were already at 4900 meters. We found a place for our tent and spent the night, going back down the next day.

We returned to our first and only camp on Kosar Gang after twenty-four hours' rest. That night was windy and cold. The weather was changing but we decided to attempt the summit regardless. It was 1500 meters above us. Denis and I were well dressed. Cory had perhaps overestimated the thermal rating of his boots. His feet started to get cold within a few hours. At 5300 meters, we had to make a decision regarding our route. Denis would have chosen one; Cory and I, another. We settled on the latter and Denis was glad of it in the end, recognizing it as the more logical and appropriate choice.

The snow was pretty deep but stable enough to walk on. The wind and cold were worsening, however. At 5800 meters, Cory could no longer feel his feet—he was freezing cold. I told him not to worry, that we would all go down, that freezing ourselves during acclimatization wasn't worth it.

I know Denis. I can tell what he's thinking by looking in his eyes. I can guess what words (and profanity) he's holding back. When I told him we'd better go down, he looked up toward the summit and said, "Okay. If that's your decision, I'll go along with it." He didn't agree at all—his tone made that crystal clear. And since Denis knew why I'd made that decision, well, it was obvious that Cory would have to work very hard in the coming weeks to earn Denis's friendship and respect.

We lost 4000 meters of altitude that day. From 5800 meters, we set out for Camp 1, struck it, and gathered all the gear on our way back to base camp. Didar and Saeed Jan had made us something to eat and drink. In the end, I decided it would be best to head down to the road at 2200 meters and travel to Skardu. I thought spending some time in relative comfort would cheer everyone up and diffuse any tension between Denis and Cory. Memory tends to favor the positive once you're out of a difficult situation, and being completely relaxed makes you less critical as well.

All of our supplies and base-camp gear arrived the next day via porter and jeep, and the the entire team was reunited. Though acclimatization was only partially complete, it was still sufficient for flying to base camp on Gasherbrum II at 5000 meters.

Years of experience have taught me that organizing an approach with a caravan of porters is very risky and often disastrous, especially when it comes to the Baltoro Glacier. It's truly a superhuman effort for the porters to walk uphill for seven days and then downhill for four, all while exposed to the winter conditions of the Karakoram. Providing them with adequate gear (which would take almost a truckload of stuff) is useless because they only sell it; and after three days of trekking they get so cold they bolt for home. What's more, the snow cover is often waist-deep, which slows progress so much that an approach requires two weeks instead of one, with the resulting depletion of food and stove fuel necessary to maintain the entire caravan. In winter, the porters have to divvy up at least one and a half metric tons of supplies. Since the maximum weight carried by each man is fifteen kilos, that means at least a hundred porters are required. A good six hundred kilos are kerosene alone, enough to fuel the stoves for a couple of months. The rest of the weight is made up of the mess tent and other expedition materials like pots, mountaineering equipment, ropes, clothing, boots, batteries, and technological instruments. And all of this for just a three-person expedition, even a light one. In a classic expedition, the total weight can double, even triple.

Transporting all of the necessary material for scaling Gasherbrum II would have required 150 porters, whose winter rates are four times higher than summer rates. Adding in the cost of our supplies, the total would have approached fifteen thousand dollars. And then the risk of losing porters due to frostbite or other illness had to be factored in. On top of all that, the inevitable bad weather would have blocked the caravan's progress for a day or two, resulting in higher daily expenses.

Yet another consideration is the environmental impact that 150 men would have on the Baltoro Glacier as they carried out their daily business. Plus, each porter consumes half a liter to a liter of kerosene per day for warmth and cooking. Multiply this by the number of porters and number of days and it comes to almost two thousand liters.

Over the years, I've learned to be pragmatic and clearheaded when considering the best way of getting to base camp, to weigh the pros and cons from the point of view of logistics, the environment, human concerns, and also the media. Some decisions can't be made impulsively or in poetic terms but rather must be based on reason. A healthy dose of realism and mature awareness clarified things: using porters would be much riskier, more polluting, and more costly than hiring a helicopter. With only two hours' flight (one in, another out) our expedition would consume less kerosene, be easier on the environment, and mitigate the porters' risk of frostbite and other problems.

January 10 was our lucky day. We boarded the military helicopter at the base of Skardu and headed for Gasherbrum II base camp at last. G2 shares a base camp with Gasherbrum I, near a permanent military base. The tale of the rarely discussed war between India and Pakistan would take a whole book to tell. It has gone on for decades, with troops permanently deployed along the contested border. This Pakistani military base at 6400 meters (the same altitude as a Camp 2 on an 8000er) is the highest in the world. There, twenty-five soldiers rotate through fifteen-day shifts all year round, winter included.

Soldiers point rifles at their "colleagues" in the darkness and freezing cold of winter at 6400 meters. Knowing that should make you think, and think a lot. But war is a business on which many economies are based, none of which, evidently, finds peace between India and Pakistan convenient. Let's not forget, these two countries were one and the same until August 14, 1947. Though geopolitical analysis is not my expertise, I've gotten to know this world while traveling to climb mountains, and I find the same problems arise almost everywhere with very little variation.

The flight from Skardu to base camp was fantastic. After forty minutes we made a stopover at the military base at Paju (3425 m). From there we continued in two stages up to base camp at 5000 meters, carrying all of our gear along. Before leaving Skardu I'd visited the pilots and the colonel in charge of the local helicopter unit. Thanks to my experience as a pilot, we struck up a friendship. It also didn't hurt that the pilots wanted to show off their skills by pushing the limits of the aircraft as far as cargo weight, altitude, and temperature were concerned. Between that and our rapport, we were able to optimize our trips and therefore the costs.

Paju, at the edge of the Baltoro Glacier, is the last place where you can find soil and shrubs. The military base is an encampment of tents and stone structures, helicopter landing pads, and endless drums of kerosene in various sizes. Military posts at higher elevations are resupplied from there.

On our second and final trip, we got out of the helicopter at 5000 meters. As soon as it lifted off the glacier, the cold, isolation, and sheer beauty of the wild Karakoram sunk in. It was already 3:00 p.m., so we didn't have enough time to site our base camp and set up. The soldiers at the outpost there were friendly and hospitable, welcoming us with tea and food. This was a rare thing, because usually, in the summer, the base is off-limits and they keep expeditions away in not altogether friendly ways.

During the six months of their obligatory stay at the outpost, the soldiers live in grimy and malodorous igloos of once-white plastic. They wear jackets, pants, and shoes, also originally white for camouflage. You can guess how long they've been there from how gray their clothing is. Officers live in more or less the same conditions as the soldiers, holed up in a few square meters, killing time, rarely washing, and going outside only during rare moments of sunshine. They stay in contact with other outposts via radio or, in exceptional cases, satellite phone. There's no TV, just a few portable radios, one or two computers for the officers, and a couple of weatherworn solar panels supplying minimal power.

It's truly difficult for the soldiers staying up there, idle, in complete solitude. Their only diversion is the helicopter. It goes through every ten days to resupply the outpost at 6400 meters with food and kerosene, leaving some nonalcoholic drinks and newspapers along the way. We were no doubt a colorful novelty.

In fact, we felt somewhat well connected. We had arrived in their helicopter, and their colonel had announced his approval via radio. Colonel Rashid Ullah Baig, a famous high-ranking army official, had given us his valuable and irreplaceable help as well. Baig was famous for having carried out the helicopter rescue of Slovenian climber Tomaž Humar when he was stuck on the Rupal Face of Nanga Parbat. That historic rescue, the first of its kind in Pakistan, had launched Baig's illustrious career.

We took shelter in the igloos as well, making space among boots, dirty sleeping bags, and blankets. We soon fell asleep thanks to the warmth of the stoves and our full stomachs—and maybe also to the level of carbon monoxide. Only Denis refused these lodgings and quickly set up a little tent. These conditions were typical of army outposts, and given that Denis is ex-military, perhaps he'd had his fill of sleeping in such places and breathing noxious fumes.

The weather was still good the next day, a rarity, and we gave the base camp setup our all. I found a deep rift between the glacier and a series of ice towers commonly called sails.

We wouldn't get much sun in there, but it would provide precious shelter from wind and storms, so we all got to work. Didar, the cook, was suffering from the altitude, while his assistant Saeed Jan, a six-foot-two giant, worked like a bulldozer. We erected the mess tent first, then the supply tent, and finally one tent each for Denis, Cory, and me. We also resumed the job of transporting all our supplies from the landing site near the military igloos to our camp 300 meters away. Surprisingly, the soldiers gave us a hand, perhaps thanks to the intercession of our cook. Knowing he could count on my approval, he had promised them some chicken and other food from our pantry in exchange for their help.

When we finished moving everything it was already late afternoon, so I invited the soldiers to hang out in our tent for some tea and cookies. Didar and Saeed Jan made a huge supper that night. The generator was working well and we didn't have to use kerosene for the lamps, so we weren't using up the oxygen inside the tent. By way of thanks, I invited the soldiers to visit regularly to check their email or call their families. Pakistanis play with their phones a lot. They download music, clips of popular dances, family photos. Having the chance to recharge their tech gadgets is very appreciated.

For a few years now, communications and technology have been the subject of vehement, specious, and often rude attacks from a small but vocal contingent of imbeciles. These people would have exploration done silently, sufferingly, heroically, almost theatrically, while the story goes untold. Obviously, I've never seen these people on a mountain in winter, or even in a normal training situation for that matter. Their butts are safe and warm as they write and speak. They're annoying, blathering on and lecturing on blogs and various forums. Yet none have written me directly, on my site. I know that criticism is the inevitable price of celebrity, but I've always naively thought that criticism should be given maturely, objectively, thoughtfully. Well, that's not how it is. In response to my intelligent suggestions of "change the channel!" and "ignore me!" some people prefer to spend minutes, hours, or indeed entire days writing colossal BS, often fueled by envy and resentment.

As usual, just as with Makalu and almost every other expedition I have chosen to share, there was someone following my Gasherbrum II expedition who criticized my having a satellite connection and thus the possibility of communicating with the outside world. As if those chunks of battery-operated plastic rendered the cold less intense and the danger virtual.

Denis, Cory, and I set out two days later for our first exploration of the Baltoro Glacier. Seracs cut off access to the upper reaches of that long tongue shared by the two Gasherbrums. Our mission was to find a way up through those seracs. Gasherbrum II may be only the thirteenth highest of the fourteen 8000-meter peaks, but the crevasse-riddled glacier defending it is among the most dangerous of all. We verified that by personal experience. A dozen times, we took turns plunging into one or another of those fissures. Only the belay rope prevented a potentially fatal incident. We used it constantly for the duration of the expedition.

On January 13, we reached the glacier's midpoint. We marked the passage through the labyrinth with high-visibility red flags on bamboo markers. Back in base camp by evening, we were satisfied yet fully conscious of the perils of the lower part of the mountain, which we'd have to face each and every time.

All the international expeditions were at their own base camps, save the one attempting Gasherbrum I—they would have arrived at our same base camp. The closest was the Polish camp on Broad Peak, guided by Artur Hajzer. That camp was only half a day's walk from us, in summertime.

Two days later, the three of us set out again and this time we were able to climb through the seracs and come out above them. We fixed only two lengths of rope, at the three steepest and most dangerous points, and that gave us great satisfaction. Cory often filmed us crossing crevasses and skirting seracs. Other times, we filmed him in action.

The weather was deteriorating but we still had some hours of light, so we continued exploring the upper part of the field of seracs. Then we turned around and headed for the base of Gasherbrum II.

We reached 5500 meters and decided to make a supply cache there. That upper region was deceptively flat and homogenous. Dangerous crevasses were laid like traps beneath a thin layer of snow. I remember slipping into a couple of them. I wasn't alone in meeting that fate, nor was I the only one to give myself quite a scare. We returned to base camp, once again crossing the labyrinth of ice. Our teeth were chattering a bit from fatigue and also from our bodies' inadequate heat generation and temperature regulation caused by imperfect acclimatization.

We rested in base camp for only two days because the weather was really terrible. Despite the sheltered position of our camp, frighteningly strong gusts forced us to batten down all of the tents with rope and chunks of ice, not to mention that the temperature was easily pushing –30 degrees Celsius. Our only refuge was the mess tent. It was covered by two or three layers of tarp anchored to the ice, which retained some of the heat radiated by the always-burning stoves. The price for that bit of comfort was kerosene-infused air and stalactites of ice hanging from the ceiling.

After those two hellish days the wind gave us a break, although the weather remained unstable. Denis, Cory, and I got up for breakfast. We decided to continue exploring and opening the access route to the upper portion of the glacier. Cory wasn't well. Nothing serious, but I thought it best to advise him to stay behind and rest in the relative warmth of base camp.

So it was just Denis and me. The route through the seracs was by now familiar, as this was our third passage. Our relative level of acclimatization made us faster. We reached the supply cache, collected everything, and headed deeper into the valley. The seven Gasherbrums completely surrounded us, with the route to base camp our only way out of that embrace. Gasherbrum was once thought to mean "shining wall" in the Balti language, and these giants are indeed cloaked in an endless glittering mantle of ice and snow. The pitches of vertical rock common to other mountain groups are uncharacteristically absent.

We were two little dots on an ice expanse of various forms and contrasting shades, ice that was hiding insidious dangers.

That day we worked hard. The snow often came up to our knees. In some places it was thigh- or even waist-deep. We hadn't brought snowshoes so we were forced to make a titanic effort to gain little ground. Denis and I both fell into deep crevasses that day as well. We saved each others' lives thanks to the rope and excellent reflexes.

The hours passed. Our progress was slowed further by having to backtrack often in order to thread our way through the maze of crevasses that seemed to show up everywhere. At least the weather wasn't too bad so we were able to work effectively.

We'd wanted to reach Camp 1 at 6000 meters but didn't get that far. We made camp at 5700 meters in the only place that seemed secure and well away from crevasses and seracs. Our little yellow tent was surrounded by a sea of gaping maws and chasms. It was like being aboard a toy boat afloat on a lake of ice.

It was a frigid night. A frozen crust of condensation formed inside the tent. It flaked off at the slightest movement and fell onto our sleeping bags and faces. Being slapped awake by ice in the face and then feeling it melt on your neck and drip down under your sweater is most definitely an awful experience.

The next morning the weather seemed good. We quickly melted some snow, ate a frugal breakfast, and were outside within minutes, striking camp and loading everything onto our backs. After tying in, we calculated the distances and resumed climbing. We were alert and ready to arrest a fall if either of us should run afoul of one of the umpteen hidden crevasses. Suddenly, when we were beneath Gasherbrum IV, the fresh snow gave way to the hard surface of an old avalanche. It would make for fast progress. Many ominous seracs hung above us. We were surrounded by seemingly bottomless crevasses. Nevertheless, it was the only route we could even dream of taking.

We hastily crossed that section to a position outside the fall line of any avalanches or seracs. The snow there was once again deep and soft. Walking through it was an ordeal, made worse by the sky completely clouding over and the winds picking up once again.

We steadily planted bamboo flags every 50 or 100 meters, like a trail of bread crumbs. Every so often I turned to look back so I could verify that the route was well marked and double-check against location and distance from landmarks. That day was dense with risk and effort. It ended at last with our arrival at Camp 1. We were nearly swimming in the snow. We placed our tent on top of a serac, in the safest possible position. We immediately got inside our haven of nylon held up by four aluminum poles and readied some food and drink. The weather was awful, with strong winds and extreme cold. But we'd made our first camp and were near Gasherbrum II and I.

We were far from base camp but not yet close enough to our mountain to start climbing it. Gasherbrum II is annoyingly protected by its smaller "siblings" and its "big brother," Gasherbrum I. So we knew that the position of our Camp 1 and the route we'd found up to it were the ultimate key to accessing G2.

We spent our second night away from base camp and our first at 6000 meters. We were feeling well and that comforted us a lot regarding our rate of adjustment to the altitude.

At the same time we were thinking of Cory, who hadn't been able to join us and now risked a deficit in his acclimatization. While we were on the mountain for those two days, Cory spent a lot of time with the soldiers and they formed an unusual friendship. He created a collection of exceptional photographs and gathered some amazing stories—unparalleled work, theretofore unknown to the media and people overseas.

On January 20, the day after we set up Camp 1, we went back to base camp. It was cloudy with low-lying fog, but it wasn't snowing and the wind had died down. Our tracks had partly disappeared. But they were replaced pretty well by flags, those fundamentally important points of reference. Everything went smoothly, apart from a few small "flights" into the usual crevasses. By nightfall we were all together once again at base camp, 5000 meters. Cory had just returned from his visit with the soldiers. The major, who was also a doctor, and another two officers had come back with him. They asked us to tell them about our two days on the mountain, and we gave them access to some electricity so they could recharge their computers and cell phones.

During our two days of rest, we contacted weather guru Karl Gabl, as always. He was almost like a fourth member of the expedition. Three days of unstable weather were on the way but not bad enough to stop us. If we dressed in the proper clothing and mustered some enthusiasm, the conditions wouldn't be prohibitive. Of course, it's all relative. We're still talking about overnight temperatures below −30 degrees Celsius, in a context of poor visibility and snowstorms. Under normal circumstances, you'd stay huddled in your sleeping bag. But when climbing in winter, weather conditions must be interpreted against the baseline reality of the season. You have to make the most of every relative change for the better.

And so we left for another reconnaissance mission higher up. Our objective was to finally set foot on Gasherbrum II and start climbing. Cory had to come if we were even to think of attempting the summit as a trio in the coming weeks. He was feeling good and had bounced back, and that set me at ease. In fact, he'd done some videos and photos and was up to carrying all of his gear himself. His relationship with Denis was developing one small step at a time without any hiccups, just at the right pace to achieve something strong and authentic.

We brought more flags with us to supplement those already in place. In the event of fog, the glacier could become a death trap. Numerous tragedies had taken place there in the past, and this was the first time anyone was venturing up there in wintertime.

Getting to Camp 1 took us half a day. Cory climbed steadily, matching our pace. He also had his first dose of plunging into crevasses, so he was now completely tuned in to the realities of Gasherbrum.

I have never understood why Gasherbrum II is considered an "easy" 8000er. Perhaps judgment is skewed by how things happen in summertime. Someone, usually local porters, prepares and marks the route and fixes ropes. The fact that twenty-odd expeditions attempt the climb each year means that the work is divided among a large number of alpinists. As a result, I suppose everything can seem easy, obvious, almost taken for granted, like a stroll for crampon-equipped trekkers. There's nothing wrong with a climb in those conditions, but the risk lies precisely in losing sight of the difficulty and the very real dangers that any mountain presents, especially an 8000er.

We were beginning to see "easy" Gasherbrum II as a decidedly tough mountain requiring all of our ability and experience. The winter season lent all the features of true exploration to the endeavor and was testing our endurance to the limit.

Like us, the neighboring expedition on Broad Peak was making the same quick and stealthy inspection of the mountain, as permitted by weather conditions. The Broad Peak expedition was larger and benefitted from the help of high-altitude porters. They, too, were equipped with satellite technology and so were able to contact us with updates of their own. Meanwhile, the two expeditions on Nanga Parbat, much easier and supposedly wilder than ours, had already given up. The Polish team had made it to Camp 1 and then closed up shop, returning to Rawalpindi and then home. The solo Russian attempt had met more or less the same fate.

Winter had thwarted the first two expeditions. For some reason, it shut down the less organized expeditions, the most "romantic" and nicest ones, the ones most pleasing to couch surfers and those nostalgic for black-and-white films.

Only two teams remained, very close together on two mountains differing in altitude by only 12 meters. It wasn't a race. Each team was attempting to write the first page of winter mountaineering history on their respective mountain and, if successful, on the whole Karakoram Range.

We woke on January 23 with our sleeping bags covered in ice. When there are three of you in a small tent, just getting out of your bag and dressing becomes a complex operation to be approached in turns, using maximum care. Otherwise, the sleeping bags get filled with ice and are therefore wet.

That day's goal was to set foot on Gasherbrum II for the first time and climb the first section, the part that showed obvious signs of avalanche activity and falling seracs. In summertime, it's avoided by staying to the left. The weather was terrible that morning, just as Karl had predicted. But making progress up the mountain was absolutely necessary in terms of acclimatization. That hour or so of what looked like an easy walk to the base of the face turned out to be nothing of the sort. We had to circumvent crevasses and travel on a section of previous avalanche, something that ignited a minor disagreement between Denis and Cory. "Shit, here we go again!" I thought. "Just when things seemed to be smoothing out."

Finally, finally—it warrants repetition—we reached that blessed cone of snow at the base of a steep couloir leading to one of the route's first shoulders. The first section was delicate, because the snow cone covered the bergschrund before nosing upward. Denis went first, then me, then Cory. We took turns leading when we came to a traverse and a narrower, steeper section leading directly to the base of a serac—at least it wasn't hanging over our heads.

While climbing, I spotted a red rope embedded under at least 5 centimeters of ice. I had the strange feeling that this unused, hibernating rope was anchoring me. But in fact I was hanging from just a few centimeters of ice ax blade, balancing precariously on crampon points. I had to dig the rope out. I swung my ax into the ice on either side of the rope with surgical precision, gradually breaking the ice while being careful not to sever the rope. That job took more than an hour. My hands and my shoulder were aching, but I managed to exhume 50 crucial meters of rope that would be useful both for ascending and descending. This earned me praise from Denis and Cory, who were in agreement with the importance of that job done. The two of them, despite their dispute 200 meters below, were sussing each other out, talking, getting to know each other, and I hoped that this climb would help them realize that they weren't incompatible but rather complementary.

At last we reached the top of an overhang with a serac on the right, which was much more stable than I expected. On the left rose a blade of ice and snow known as Gasherbrum II's Banana Ridge. It was too late to start climbing it, and the weather showed no sign of improving. I suggested we make a temporary camp just beneath the serac, at 6250 meters, and my companions agreed, partly because it was an obvious choice. We talked a lot that night and joked about a lot of little details, and I sensed that the dangers we were facing together were increasing team cohesion.

During the night, the wind didn't let up on our tent. The only barrier between us and the freezing cold outside was one thin layer of nylon. Still, it was enough to make us feel protected. We slept squashed together in an attempt to keep warm and prayed for better weather in the morning.

Our prayers were partially answered. The weather was still pretty bad the next day, but at least the wind had died down. We clambered up the Banana with great care, clinging by the steel points of our crampons and ice axes. The ice was hard. Pieces of rope abandoned by previous expeditions poked out of it here and there. We tried to splice them all together, but in the end we just stayed tied in to our own rope. It took a whole day to get past those 250 meters of lofty ice. To me, climbing the Banana seemed like climbing on the rim of an ear cocked toward the emptiness.

Finally, we were almost out of the Banana. Denis, who was in front at that point, had to use his ice ax as an anchor. Cory and I climbed up his rope, slowly. We were huffing and puffing from the weight of our packs and the huge effort that front-pointing demanded of our calf muscles. Once I got to Denis, he was satisfied and pointed to his anchor.

"Simone, I'll have to leave the ax behind. There's no other secure anchor point. I tried digging but didn't find any ice!"

"Okay, take it easy. I'll lead. This blade of compact snow is going to be tricky, but if I manage to get up there, this damned Banana should be over with."

Denis belayed me while Cory climbed up the rope that Denis had tied to the ax. The first few meters were pretty simple, but once the ridge pitched upward I felt like I was moving on nothingness, as though I were climbing a mound of icing sugar. I had to proceed with maximum delicacy and sensitivity, flat-footing and keeping all my weight perpendicular to the slope. I'm sure that Denis would have arrested my fall had it happened, but the pendulum would have been 40 meters. I wouldn't have gotten out of it with a simple scare—more likely with fractures.

I maintained a steady pace and constant focus, locking any thoughts of falling or making a mistake out of my head. I had to move on that sugary snow and pack it as best I could. Just then, something came back to me from a different time and place, an experience I'd had on the tricky section of a grade 10 slab with the next piece of protection far away. Making that connection in my mind helped a lot.

I don't know how much time passed, but I'm guessing it wasn't much. Finally, I took the last four steps, the most treacherous ones, and then hopped over a bump and onto the final shoulder of that extremely long

Banana. From there, I went along practically hugging that blade of snow until I found myself on top of the hump, lying on my belly. I flipped myself over, caught my breath, and then got to my feet. I plunged my ice ax in to the hilt, tied the rope to it, and yelled down, "Denis! Come on up! We're there!"

He raised his arms by way of acknowledgment and celebration. Cory lifted his ax in a wave and then waited for Denis to complete his traverse on the rope I'd just fixed.

Soon, they both reached me. Twenty meters below us, we spotted a wide, secure rise on which to set up our Camp 2 tent, so we rappeled down to it. The weather during the past few hours had been brutal, really ugly, almost as if to punish us for daring to venture this far up.

We quickly set up camp and performed the usual ritual: one of us dashes into the tent, another knocks snow off of the packs and passes them in, and the third collects ice. Within fifteen minutes we were all stuffed inside the tent, still wearing our high-altitude suits and mountaineering boots. You can tell a team's level of cohesion by its ability to accept the following scenario: Putting up with elbows to the ribs while the first person undresses, unstuffs his sleeping bag, and gets into it on one side of the tent. Then, while the last person waits patiently, the second removes his boots, exposing wet and steaming socks that he passes to his neighbor, who arranges them under his head like a pillow or maybe spreads them out on his empty pack. Once the second person is finally lying in his own sleeping bag, he's out of the way (if you can call it that). The third person keeps his high-altitude suit on and melts snow while asking the others what they want for supper.

That day the team got top marks on its final exam. We were fast, friendly, playful, cooperative. We ate the goulash my wife had prepared before the expedition, drank copious amounts of liquids—in this, Cory was unbeatable—and finally the cook (Denis) got into his sleeping bag for the night.

Eating good, tasty food instead of poisoning yourself with freeze-dried packets that all taste the same is a trick I learned from the Polish. Economic straits coupled with a good dose of wisdom compelled them to prepare and vacuum-seal their meals in advance. And indeed, eating stew and real potatoes, or goulash with polenta made by my wife, is much better than swallowing freeze-dried nutrition that you can't even recognize unless you read the ingredients. Tortellini, parmesan cheese, small salamis, smoked prosciutto, cookies, snacks, *torrone*, cola-flavored or mint candies, wafers, chocolate spread, jams, and so on formed the bulk of our diet on Gasherbrum II, just as they had for years on all of my expeditions. As for the goulash, I recall going to the butcher shop with my brother-in-law two days before leaving for the expedition. It was located in the South Tyrol, in Anterivo, a town of 250 souls. The three kilos of meat I purchased had been locally raised and slaughtered. The shop is a few meters square. Mr. Mattivi, the owner, has cheeks as rosy as his flavorful steaks, the nose of a grappa lover, and last but not least, the winking eye of a Romeo. Eating meat from his shop and tasting the flavors of home always has an energizing effect on my body and mind.

That night we slept well enough despite the altitude and cramped quarters. We tried to keep each other warm and all move at the same time into the same position. The night slipped (icily) by.

The next morning, I triggered a snowfall of condensation while trying to unzip the tent for a look outside. My companions told me where to go in no uncertain terms. But they liked me again once I gave them the happy news: the weather was beautiful, a bluebird day, with barely any wind.

"Really? Wow. That's a good thing," said Denis.

"Great," said Cory, and rolled over.

To tease him, I roughed him up through his sleeping bag and he burst out laughing.

Our plan for that day, January 26, was to go back to base camp. The clear sky gave us wings. However, the temperature was still hovering around thirty to forty below and it wouldn't warm up until the sun hit us. Clapping our hands, windmilling our arms, and wiggling our toes like crazy inside our boots were all automatic by now.

We climbed back up to the col 20 meters above our camp and retraced our steps on the Banana, occasionally lowering ourselves on some lengths of rope but for the most part downclimbing with our axes and crampons. Denis and I left our axes as anchors up at 6100 meters, and Cory did the same in the end for the last long rappel down onto the glacier. From there we followed our flags and our half-hidden wind-blown tracks through the endless labyrinth. Despite all that, we weren't spared a few tumbles into crevasses. Still, we got down quite smoothly and quickly, all things considered. Seeing Didar, Saeed Jan, and Hassan was a great pleasure once again. Even the grimy military post seemed warm and inviting.

That same afternoon, our military friends came back for a visit. We had a pleasant time. We shared a snack, talked about our climb, and the officer/doctor managed to Skype his father who was working in the United Arab Emirates. The tranquil vibe was somewhat spoiled that evening when we read the Polish expedition's website. They had encountered extreme cold and winds unfit for humans, a frozen hell. Meanwhile, fortune had favored us. Yet we'd been practically on the same mountain, in the identical valley, during the very same winter! Maybe they had an inkling of our steady progress, even though it hadn't been emphasized in our communication. On a human level, I understood their disappointment, but the envy they expressed toward us clashed with what I had thought was a friendly rapport. We were all in the Karakoram and were all suffering through the same terrible conditions. Our teams and strategies differed but the weather and temperature certainly didn't.

During our three days of rest at base camp, bad weather put our camp's endurance to the test, forcing us to work constantly at anchoring the tents and tarps. At times we even had to brace and hold up the poles ourselves to prevent the mess tent from being swept away. And I thought the Patagonian winds had no equal! Just go to the Karakoram in winter and you'll find winds to rival them.

The third day, I called Karl Gabl.

"Ciao, Karl! How's it going?"

"Everything's fine here, thanks. It's you I'm wondering about. How are you making out? I heard that you got to 6400 meters. Well done!"

"Yes, Karl, thanks! We're at base camp resting and waiting for our moment. Can you give us a forecast?"

"Yes, sure. Call me in an hour."

Karl's kindness and availability know no bounds. I've called him at the most unimaginable times and during the most sacred of holidays. I even called him at a very inopportune time once, for which I apologized profusely. His wife had just passed. My wife and I had met her once over dinner. Even at that difficult time, Karl had given me a weather report.

One hour later, we were back on the satellite phone.

"Hi, Karl, what's the scoop?"

"I only see one break in the weather, Simone. A thirty-hour window, I repeat, thirty hours, three days from now! Before and after that, the weather will be like it is now. Actually, it looks as though after that, things will get worse."

"Are there any other possible windows? Maybe farther off?"

"You know I don't make forecasts more than five to seven days ahead. You can't trust them. Besides, the numbers aren't showing anything good."

I paused to think for a few seconds before answering. "Okay, Karl. I guess that means we leave tomorrow. If the window is so small and it arrives in three days, I'll want to be at Camp 2 when it starts, so we can make the summit attempt during those thirty favorable hours."

"You know I never tell you what to do, Simone. I only told you about these thirty hours because I know you'll use your head and stick to the plan, like you did on Makalu. Do what you think is right but remember, it'll be hell again afterward."

"Thanks, Karl. I'll talk it over with Denis and Cory. I'll bring the satellite phone and call you every day for updates."

"I'll be here. Good luck!"

Denis and Cory had been with me and had guessed the content of the call from hearing my side of the conversation.

"We have to go, guys, we have to go tomorrow! There's a thirty-hour window and it could be the right one, maybe the only one."

"Okay, Simone. What time?"

"No need to rush. Let's say between eight and nine."

It took only minutes to make the decision that bore the full weight of our summit dream. Like in an action movie, an inevitable countdown would begin in three days' time. Before then, though, we would have to climb for two days through a storm, trusting solely to our abilities and Karl's forecast.

On January 30, we ventured out into the insane wind and cold. We aimed to arrive at Camp 1. The route somehow seemed familiar and less inhospitable even though we'd only done it twice before. Everything went smoothly, apart from having cold hands. Cory felt it most intensely because he had to wear gloves rather than the warmer mittens, in order to photograph and film. Just before Camp 1, Denis did a swan dive into a gigantic crevasse. We were alarmed by it, partly because it seemed strange that the glacier could have moved and opened up that much in the span of so few days.

We arrived at the Camp 1 tent at about 2:00 p.m. Visibility was extremely poor and the wind had already drifted snow over the top of our little yellow nylon shelter. Following the usual procedures and division of labor, we got into the tent and fired up the stove right away for some warmth, knowing full well that it would coat the inside of the tent with a layer of frozen condensation.

We teased Denis a little for his flight into the crevasse. It relieved the tension and lent some semblance of normalcy to our making an attempt on the summit so soon after arrival at base camp.

Wind gusts woke us a dozen times during the night. In the morning we were all fine and so we got going again, knowing what awaited us: the long, flat stretch of glacier between Gasherbrum I and II, then the ramp, the narrow couloir, a break at the serac, the tricky climb of the Banana, and lastly, the sharp ridge to Camp 2 at 6400 meters. We took turns leading, with Cory filming and photographing nonstop. His job was a constant and meticulous one, truly admirable given the weather conditions. Denis and I had prepared some anchors to substitute for the three ice axes we'd left behind, since we needed to retrieve them. The anchors were nothing fancy, but definitely effective. We'd found a bamboo cane at base camp, about 8 centimeters in diameter. We'd cut it, pierced a hole so a small rope could pass through, and held it all together with tape to make it solid.

The wind and cold made that day's climb punishing, but we managed to arrive at Camp 2. Hardly needing to speak, we swiftly executed the ritual procedures. This time, Cory offered to collect the ice and get in last. He took the opportunity to capture that moment in video and pictures as well.

Cory and Denis had become friends by this point. Denis had finished his personal "test" of his new friend. He'd challenged Cory, observed him, chewed him out, and now treated him almost as a brother. He admired the seriousness and professionalism that Cory brought to his work of documenting everything. Cory in turn told us he'd never had climbing partners who had returned the favor by offering to capture him on film as well. That day, as soon as he got into the tent, he exclaimed, "Thanks guys! I think this is the first time I'll go home with some footage that includes me as well!"

After eating and drinking, it was time to call Karl.

"Hi, Karl. It's Simone. We're at Camp 2. We're happy to be here, we're doing well, even though it was two days of hell, like you said."

"Well done! I was waiting for your call. I can confirm the good weather window starting early tomorrow morning. Listen, don't forget. There's only about thirty hours. Then a scary wind will blow through, with gusts up to 140 kilometers per hour."

"Okay, Karl. Thanks for the good news. We'll be careful, we'll go for it!"

"Good luck, Simone. Say hi to Denis and Cory for me."

My companions had figured out that Karl had confirmed his fore-cast, and our faces all lit up with smiles.

"Guys, tomorrow we'll get up early but we won't leave until the sun reaches us. We'll aim for 6900 meters. The clear skies will mean lower temperatures and we don't want anyone to freeze. From there on, we have 1700 meters to do alpine-style, with none of us having set foot up there this year. So it'll be an unknown for all of us. We have only thirty hours. You know it as well as I do, or better. We can try it . . . actually, we can *do* it, but we have to stay united and help each other, even if only by encouraging each other."

The next day, when we saw the sun shining in a blue sky, our morale soared despite the wind and cold. Karl was right again. That darned Gabl. How does he manage to be so infallible?

The climb proved complicated right from the start (wait, doesn't everyone say Gasherbrum II is easy?). Shortly after leaving Camp 2, we came across two seracs. They were tough to overcome because the bergschrund at their base was covered in snow—we had to wade through it to get to the tops of the seracs.

We did our best to execute the necessary maneuvers, taking turns, while Cory captured it all. We proceeded quickly, with an eye always on the sky, on the horizon. Thirty hours aren't many, and we knew they would pass quickly.

We ground out meter after meter, overcoming seracs and crevasses, traveling on sections of hard ice and others of mixed. It was heavy going and every meter had to be earned. The sun hadn't brought any actual warmth, unfortunately, just a dash of comfort. At the very least it guaranteed us maximum visibility and a good mood.

We didn't run into any problems. In the afternoon, we came to a hump-like serac at about 6900 meters. We all agreed it might be a good place to settle in for the night and the right place to leave from the next day in order to reach our goal. We were inside the tent in the blink of an eye. The temperature would soon plunge below –40 degrees Celsius, and it was important to be prepared when it did, with sleeping bags at the ready. While Denis started melting snow and ice for supper, I called Karl again. It was crucial that he confirm his forecast.

The phone range once, twice, three times . . .

"*Ja*, Gabl."

"Ciao, Karl, it's Simone. We can see a ton of peaks from here! We're at about 6900 meters."

"*Gut*! I reconfirm. You'll have thirty hours with this visibility, no more. It will change suddenly around noon tomorrow. Stay in control. Starting noon tomorrow, it'll be blizzard and storm."

"Okay, Karl. We'll try to play our hands and wrap up by noon, with or without the summit, I promise."

"Good luck and be careful. I'm here if you need me."

That night, despite the confirmation, we were all a bit tense. The thought of so few hours of clear skies before all hell broke loose was making us nervous. We decided to get up at 1:30 a.m.—a strange time for a winter ascent because the temperature can vary between forty and fifty below. But time was flying by and there wasn't much time to wait or rest. We had to find the courage to use every possible moment and act decisively and quickly.

We woke as scheduled. At three in the morning, we went out into the pitch black. The gelid air assaulted us immediately, striking like a punch in the nose. The collars of our high-altitude suits were iced up after very few steps. We turned on our headlamps and started our race against time. That "nearly impossible" from the previous year's winter attempt on Broad Peak was still ringing in my ears.

Despite wanting to climb quickly, we had a lot to contend with, what with the 7000 meters of altitude, the cold, and the dark. We started out aiming directly upward for the ridge. In an hour of climbing we reached a wide ridge. As we went along this spine in the dark, crevasses revealed themselves at the last possible moment. Then we encountered a rock rampart and skirted it on the right. Occasionally, we came across old pieces of frayed and useless rope. The headlamps were never bright enough, and we tried to orient ourselves by looking around in the faint starlight. The moon wasn't even out to give us a hand.

It took another hour to get around the rock pillar, and then we resumed our direct ascent. We came across another rocky section. We couldn't bypass it, so instead we tackled it head-on. All of this slowed our progress, as did the level of exposure and difficulty of the pitch ahead, which made our movements more wary and uncertain. Another hour disappeared during that stretch of mixed climbing in the pitch dark. Once at the top of the section, we regrouped. Our faces had been reduced to panting masks of ice, but we continued our climb without a word.

Time passed relentlessly. Since we were gaining altitude, there was no relief from the cold. On the rock rampart we veered to the left while the first, tentative light of dawn began broadening our field of vision.

The diagonal line of ascent to the left took us another hour. Then, finally, we were at 7450 meters. At that moment, an extraordinary yet altogether natural phenomenon occurred. The very first blessed and indescribable ray of sunlight pierced through and a band of light illuminated us, starting with Denis, then me, then Cory. It was incredible, like our faces were being gently bathed in warm water. The temperature jumped from −50 to −35 degrees Celsius within seconds. The horizon at our backs lit up with blue surrounded by orange. Chogolisa, Broad Peak, K2, the Gasherbrums, Masherbrum . . . the entire Karakoram Range was illuminated. The sky was crisp and crystalline because of the arctic temperatures. Everything seemed perfectly still but the rising sun revealed everything to be bursting with life.

Cory didn't let that moment escape. He yelled to us to stay put and surged ahead of us. Gasping for air, he threw himself on the ground, took out his reflex camera and trained his lens on us. He signaled for us to continue while he took a burst of photos and some video footage, probably the most spectacular and striking I've ever seen. When we reached him, he was still wheezing and fighting to keep his lens steady. We stretched upward and thanked the sky for those rays of sunlight showering down on us, getting stronger and warmer.

We switched off our headlamps and started a seemingly endless traverse to the right, beneath the imposing rock triangle that protects the summit. The wind-packed snow sometimes gave way under our weight, letting us sink, but most of the time it supported our rapid progress and gave our crampons good purchase.

The sun was still shining on us but its heat seemed spent. The higher we got, the stiffer the wind. Four hours remained in the countdown and the storm was building. We finally reached the end of the traverse at 7700 meters. Three hundred and fifty meters to go in four hours . . . maybe we could make it but only if we used every last second.

The long slope was ahead. We were on the Pakistan–China border, maybe even with a foot in each country. We'd been roped together since the morning. Because we were a roped team, our paces were identical.

We started up that last, lengthy section of ridge. It was mind over muscle now, a fight in the wind and the cold. We could have found thousands of reasons to quit. We were exhausted, wiped out, yet knew we still had the wherewithal to achieve our dream, to seize the so-called impossible. We were like automatons: a swing of the ax, a step, another swing, another kick of crampon points into the hard snow.

Honestly, I don't remember much of those last few hours. All I remember is being filled with an overwhelming desire to climb and enough rage to kill a polar bear with my bare hands. A million things went through my mind: people, flashes of past training sessions, thoughts that spurred me on in spite of anything or anyone. But I wasn't blind or deaf to what was happening around me. I kept looking around, trying to determine the direction from which hell would strike down on us.

We found some rope pieces of various colors and diameters. Some were flying almost like kites, others disappeared into the snow, still others were in plain sight on the surface. One of these ropes in particular has stuck in my memory. It was yellow plastic and pointed directly to a knife-edged ridge. Five meters before reaching the top, though, it disappeared into the snow. Denis took it upon himself to climb up to the point where it sank and kept going while I belayed him. Once he reached the top of the ridge and disappeared over the other side, he found a red rope hanging from above. He grabbed it and threw it down to me. I grabbed it, tied it to the yellow one and started to climb up it. I joined Denis on the ridge and looked up . . .

I could hardly believe my eyes. I could see the summit! I kept it together and signaled to Cory to climb up quickly. It was past eleven and we had one hour left in our countdown. Gasherbrum I was getting socked in, and an even bigger cloud formation was stampeding toward us like a herd of bison about to trample everyone and everything.

As soon as Cory reached us, Denis took off to climb the last length of red rope leading directly to the summit, while I belayed him. Cory had already started filming. A large knot forced Denis to stop, release the ascender, and reposition it above the blockage in order to continue.

I was next. We were now mere minutes away from the beginning of a fight between human willpower and nature's fury.

Denis came to the end of the red rope, 10 meters below the summit. I couldn't see him clearly anymore. The wind had turned stormy and was whipping up snow crystals, unleashing a flurry of razor blades on us before returning to the mountain.

Head down, I resumed counting the number of steps between breathing breaks. Three series later, I was at the end of the red rope as well. I turned to see Cory coming up at a steady pace, keeping the fixed distance between us as he climbed. I looked upward just in time to see Denis's last step up and his first step to the right onto the flat summit of Gasherbrum II. He took a couple more steps and then turned to me, arms upraised. With one last series of steps taken twice as fast as usual, I echoed the very same movements. I came to a bamboo flag planted in the snow of the summit and kneeled. I started to cough from the effort of going double-time. My spit was thick and icy and my throat dry. The coughing and spitting further reduced my flow of air, so I was gasping for air.

At last I recovered, but I stayed on my knees with my head bowed down to the snow. I thought of my father, always my father. He'd been my beacon, my lighthouse all my life. He'd been gone ten years, but I could feel him close by and I knew he was proud of me at that moment. He always supported me, never made fun of my desire to become a great mountaineer, to make my passion into a career. He never tried to quell my enthusiasm when I said I wanted to become like Messner. I was only thirteen then, but he always took me seriously, giving me advice on how to carry out my life plan while still explaining that I was gambling on a nearly impossible dream and would have to prepare for the possibility of losing that gamble.

And Gasherbrum II in winter was nearly impossible. Artur Hajzer had said as much after his 2010 Broad Peak expedition. Meanwhile, Cory had reached the summit and was hard at work with his heavy cameras, as usual.

It was 11:35 a.m. on February 2, 2011. Denis was dressed in yellow, Cory in orange, and I in red. It was a singularly beautiful, poignant, and moving moment for those three colorful dots on the summit of an 8000er in the Karakoram, the first to be there in winter.

This was a historic event, unrepeatable, like the first summit of Everest or man's first landing on the moon. We'd done it in alpine-style, something that had virtually incurred derision. But it was precisely that strategy that had been the key to success during those thirty hours, along with the determination and team spirit of three mountaineers and friends from three different continents.

Dark clouds had engulfed everything by then. I took a few pictures of Cory and Denis, even though the view wasn't that great. We also took one of our three smiling faces, and then Cory shouted, "Now we have to get the fuck out of here!" We had another unavoidable summit to conquer: getting to safety.

Spurred by Cory's invective, we started down just twenty minutes after reaching the summit. The hellish weather forecasted by Karl was just around the corner, and we began to battle for our very survival. We had to downclimb the entire route and find that route in decidedly different visibility conditions, damnably limited ones this time.

Many pitches were much more hostile on the descent, and we had to downclimb using our ice axes and crampons as though on waterfall ice. Unanchored, the fixed ropes lashed us like whips. The mountain seemed to be rebelling against those who had dared set foot on its summit in the winter. Nature was putting us through yet another test, this time to see whether we deserved to go home and share the story of our part in the history of human exploration.

We weren't entirely sure where we were, but we kept descending, trusting to the plan. Every so often we'd check in with each other and then keep going. We got to the col at 7700 meters and sheltered under an overhang. From there I made two quick calls on the satellite phone: one to my wife to tell her we'd summited and were on our way down; the other to the master, Krzysztof Wielicki, the king of winter ascents (an honor he shares with Jerzy Kukuczka). Wielicki and Piotr Pustelnik are the Polish mountaineers I respect the most: never an unnecessary word, never a hint of jealousy, never spiteful, always willing to acknowledge their colleagues' virtues along with their vices and to applaud or admonish them accordingly. I received their congratulations with great joy. I made one last call, this one to base camp. I told them we'd made it and heard joyful shouts from all present. But for us, the battle was far from over.

We crossed the border and entered Pakistan as we started the long traverse below the rocky pyramid. The sunlight and blue sky, the photos and sense of peace—these were already mere memories, swept away by shocking gusts of wind that blew us over. Fatigue had set in. We'd been going for thirteen hours by then, without any food or drink, breathing only the rarefied air of extreme altitude. Somehow we managed to make it through that traverse. We prepared to face the steepest part of our descent toward the distant Camp 3, which we'd established on our way by moving Camp 2 up. That section was difficult. We kept getting lost while trying to discern our only points of reference: the rock pillar we'd bypassed on the way up, and that wide, crevasse-infested spine. It was like watching a film in reverse while trying to conjure the most minute of details from memory. Now we were in the middle of the storm, disoriented but constantly in motion, always talking, always sticking together, and never letting each other out of sight.

That infernal descent lasted an eternity. At a certain point, we lost all sense of how far we had left to go. At one point, Denis shouted something to me. The wind was so strong that I couldn't make it out, even though I was only a few meters away. I went up to him, put my arm around his shoulders, and shouted for him to say it again.

"I glimpsed a tent down there, Simone. But it's not ours! It's a different color!"

"That's impossible. It has to be ours! Who else could be here but us?"

"It's not ours, I'm sure of it. It's green!"

"Okay, Denis. Let's head for it. Doesn't matter whose it is, it's going to save our asses!"

"Okay, okay. Let's go."

Denis forged ahead between gusts while we held onto him from the rear. I was almost on top of him at this point, trying to catch sight of a tent and make sense of what he'd said. Suddenly, we saw it, a few meters in front of us. It was yellow. Our tent.

"Yes, yes, our tent!" I shouted at the top of my lungs.

Soon we were all standing around that precious shelter. It was holding firm in the violence of the storm. We took off only our crampons and dove inside. Our faces were monstrous masks of ice, almost unrecognizable.

Once we were inside the tent, night descended and our mood improved. We exchanged congratulations but nothing more. Our top priority, after fifteen hours of uninterrupted effort, was to eat and drink and think about how to get down the next day. I called my wife again, explained the situation, downplaying the dangers we were facing as much as possible, telling her not to worry.

That night—the fourth we'd spent away from base camp—the tent was pounded by a wind that seemed to want to tear it from the mountain. Our sleeping bags were wet by then, so our high-altitude suits were our only means of warmth. We never took them off, not even at night inside our ice-stiffened sleeping bags. The tension, meanwhile, was increasing. We knew we were running the risk of being trapped up there if we didn't set out at first light.

It was 8:00 a.m. when we finished packing the tent and all the other gear. We distributed the weight evenly among us and started down. Visibility was reduced to no more than 3 or 4 meters and, as if that weren't enough, our goggles were iced up. We had to leave our eyes unprotected and resort to squinting. We no longer had easy landmarks like ridges or pillars by which to orient ourselves. We were enveloped in a gray and white cloud, with seracs and crevasses to steer clear of and straightforward traverses to execute.

That day, I gave myself the task of leading. I knew that getting lost would be fatal, so I became almost obsessed with finding the start of a rope that would lead us to the uppermost serac, the same serac we'd climbed two days before, so we could rappel down it. But the rope was white, as white as what surrounded us. How do you find a white rope in a white world during a storm?

I concentrated as hard as possible, isolating myself in a kind of parallel universe, one without sound. Paying attention to every little sign, I strove to remember the climb from two days prior. I searched for tracks and other signs of our passage. But it was all so complicated, almost impossible. There was that word again, that intolerable adjective . . .

I continued the descent and my companions followed.

I don't know how, but at some point I found myself 2 meters from the buried anchor point of a white rope that emerged from the snow and immediately disappeared in the fog right in front of me, between my feet.

I let out a shout of joy and turned to Denis and Cory.

"How the fuck did you manage that?!" they exclaimed in unison.

I didn't even answer. I didn't know what to say. I just smiled and clipped in to that magical signpost of our route. We took turns rappelling down the white rope and got past the first serac. The rope petered out after another dozen or so meters. But at that point, memory served up a few important details. We crossed a crevasse and then turned immediately left toward the ridge, a very important natural landmark.

The difficulties were considerable and we often encountered vertical ice. I placed our first ice screw and we used our rope to lower ourselves. We repeated that process a couple of times. The rope's length was unwieldy and it was difficult to find a place to wait for the others before descending another pitch. I wound up in another crevasse, but thankfully I was roped up.

That descent was quite the odyssey. The wind buffeted us to the left and right. We were disoriented, but an unshakeable survival instinct propelled and compelled us to descend, to persevere, to never give up. A combination of luck, ability, intuitive flashes, and joint decisions led us miraculously to Camp 2. When we glimpsed it, I was seized by an indescribable happiness. I felt reborn. From Camp 2, our makeshift anchors would make getting down the next hundred or so meters much easier. Once we got to the serac where we'd bivied, we would only have to find the opening of that fairly easy couloir and eventually find that red rope, the one I had dug out with my ice ax a few days before.

Nevertheless, we continued to exercise caution and restraint and to proceed in a calculated way. Things were definitely getting less difficult. Orienting ourselves was no longer an insane task, and that took a load off of us. One by one, we descended the length of the Banana and then the couloir beneath the serac. The red rope was there waiting, as though to repay me for having liberated it, for having brought it back into the light. We tied a loop into the end of the rope. I'd brought a black rope along and we threaded it through the loop. This made the rappel down to the glacier possible. We'd gotten down off of Gasherbrum II at last. Now, we began the lengthy descent of the glacier shared by G1 and G2.

Contrary to expectation, we had trouble orienting ourselves on the glacier too. Although we'd placed flags quite close together between base camp and Camp 1, between Camps 1 and 2 they were farther apart.

We walked over blocks of snow from an old avalanche. Many times, we were tempted to veer right, toward Gasherbrum V, thinking our Camp 1 tent was there. We often teetered on the verge of error and had to retrace our steps, continuing to follow the path of the avalanche. It seemed like we'd been walking a long time, yet we hadn't even reached the detour toward the serac on which we'd pitched our tent. We wasted a lot of time before finally finding the green flag that indicated where a 90-degree turn would line us up directly with Camp 1. Evening was approaching, so we dropped the idea of continuing on toward base camp and prepared to spend the night at Camp 1.

We were most definitely fatigued, worn out. The prospect of facing yet another (the sixth!) day of climbing didn't exactly fill us with cheer. We threw ourselves into the tent and then got some food and drink ready. We'd been paying constant attention to nutrition and hydration because the quality of our effort depended largely on our caloric intake. Cory was the most careful about hydration. He constantly urged us to follow his example. Our "official photographer" had had to give up on his reflex camera, which had stopped working at 7700 meters due to the cold and blizzard. He'd switched to using my compact professional one—he found its quality and resolution satisfactory.

Time passed slowly that night at Camp 1. We didn't feel much like talking. Our sleeping bags were blocks of ice. The zippers were tough to open or didn't open at all. So we slept outside of them, huddled together, hoping morning would come quickly and bring clearer weather.

Once again, Karl Gabl had been right. The weather conditions were terrible, unrelentingly bloody awful, and yet I don't recall suffering the cold that night any more than any other. Perhaps the increased oxygen level, and therefore our increased ability to generate body heat, made up for the lack of a sleeping bag.

After our usual quick, frugal breakfast of tea and the last of our cookies, we exited the tent. We had just started our last morning on Gasherbrum II. The comforts of base camp awaited us; then our celebration and return home.

We left Camp 1 around 8:00. Right away, we noticed the effects of all that wind and storm. All of the snow had been swept off the slopes and deposited at their bases. In short, we would be up to our hips in snow. It was truly an ordeal, the ultimate torture. We could see the flags sticking out of the snow cover, but there was no way to tell where our tracks had been. Deviating just 20 centimeters to the left or right of our buried path would sink us twice as deep in snow. I tried to probe the snow with my trekking pole, but it was very slow going, requiring both sensitivity and luck. We were hobbling along, exhausted. We took turns leading, switching regularly. Still, we were practically moving in slow motion. The flags were a comforting point of reference but could prove dangerous. Heading straight for them, as we were now doing, we risked running afoul of crevasses that we'd previously avoided by detouring.

Somehow we managed to get to the point below Gasherbrum V where we had passed quickly over an avalanche trail during the ascent. That blocky, solid terrain had given way to at least 60 centimeters of powder snow. In short, we were now at the most dangerous part of our descent—and, based on how slowly we were going, it was going to take us a long time to get through it. But there was no other way to get to the red flag marking the spot where we would turn left and begin crossing the crevasses and clefts that lay between us and the top of the serac field. From there we would be able to see the military post.

We had no choice. We could only hope that nothing would release from the loaded slopes of Gasherbrum V, that no seracs would topple...

I was literally swimming in snow, lungs exploding with the effort. Denis decided to relieve me. I went to the back, behind Cory. Denis made a superhuman effort to move forward quickly, but our advance remained extremely, distressingly slow.

Denis and I kept looking upward to our right, keeping an eye on the slope. At a certain point we heard a boom, a terrible noise, almost an explosion, and witnessed the collapse and fall of a serac onto the overloaded slope beneath it, which, with another boom, began to pour directly down toward us at breakneck speed. It was an avalanche of awesome proportions, and incredibly fast. Using every scrap of air in our lungs, Cory and I yelled in unison, "Avalaaaaaaanche!"

Denis, deeply focused as he was on finding our route, didn't even hear us, or perhaps had a delayed reaction. I tried to flee, a ridiculous attempt given that all three of us were hip-deep in fresh powder. Cory and I managed to move maybe about a meter before that enormous, accelerating bulk was on top of us.

Hassan, Saeed Jan, and Didar were at base camp inside the mess tent. They hadn't heard from us in three days. They'd followed the weather developments and knew it was almost impossible to survive so long out there. Didar, who'd known me for nearly ten years, had tried to calm everyone, but by then he probably wasn't even sure himself what to expect.

It was 10:15 a.m. The three of them were huddled silently around the stoves, with the tent unzipped for some fresh air. A black crow with a red beak appeared suddenly at the opening. Completely fearless, he hopped into the mess tent, cocked his head at them, and loudly cawed. The three Pakistanis were gobsmacked. He stood there a few minutes, staring at them, and then hopped back to the exit and flew off.

Hassan jumped out of his chair and yelled, "Something's happened, guys, something's gone wrong!"

Didar and Saeed Jan always took Hassan seriously. He was their elder and more experienced.

"What should we do?" asked Saeed Jan.

"Let's make a thermos of tea and some food, get a bottle of cola from the soldiers, and head out to meet Simone, Denis, and Cory!"

Saeed Jan made this happen at lightning speed and started out without crampons or rope, in just his high mountaineering boots. Hassan followed close behind, asking Didar to wait at base camp, ready to execute any orders to come.

It was 10:15 a.m. when the avalanche swept us away, when everything went dark and we began to whirl over and over along with blocks of ice and snow. All of us were wearing big packs, and we were traveling as a roped team, a very dangerous thing under those conditions. Often everyone ends up suffering the same fate as the least lucky member of the team, the one who gets most deeply buried. Or the rope could wrap around someone's neck, strangling the poor soul.

Immersed in snow, I was conscious. I felt repeated jerks pulling me upward. In turn, I pulled one of my two companions upward, not having a clue which one of them it was. All the while, I kept frantically treading water as though trying to stay afloat. I never fought against the avalanche's roiling; rather, I went along with it, attempting to stay on the surface. There was a sensation of being in a vacuum, then another two or three tumbles and rolls . . . and then everything stopped.

The next few seconds felt like an eternity. It would be months before each of us shared what we saw, heard, and felt in those interminable moments.

When I opened my eyes, I found myself almost free of the avalanche, sitting only up to my ankles in snow. My mitts were gone and I had snow everywhere, but I was okay. I understood immediately that I had been spared, that nothing was broken, and that I had to look for my friends. A fear crept in that they hadn't survived, that they had met the same fate as Anatolij and Dimitri on Annapurna in 1997 . . .

Eventually, though, I caught sight of Cory's orange suit and then his head popping up out of the snow. I took off my pack and sped toward him. I stroked his face and told him to stay calm, and then I began madly digging with my hands, which were protected only by the thin glove liners of my lost mitts.

Panting, I dug without pause, terrified that the snow would harden around him. Meanwhile, I kept looking around for Denis. Finally I saw the black hood of his Gore-Tex jacket just barely peeking out of the snow. I shouted his name and he responded immediately, "Okay, okay, Simone, I'm okay, take your time."

I kept digging until I had freed one of Cory's arms, then the other. After that he started to dig himself. Within a few seconds, he opened the zipper of his high-altitude suit, pulled out his camera, and started to film and take photographs.

I jumped up and flew toward Denis. He was more deeply buried than Cory had been, but his mouth was above the snow and he was breathing regularly. I couldn't feel my hands anymore, they were frozen, but I couldn't and wouldn't stop. I dug like a madman and managed to get an arm down under Denis's underarm. I tried to pull him out, but he didn't budge.

Cory, obviously in shock, had captured it all, even himself in tears, and now was digging his legs out with his hands.

At last I uncovered Denis up to his sternum, but it would be another ten minutes before he could use his free arm to dig along with me. He was in a very uncomfortable position, and his pack anchored him in the progressively hardening snow. Once his other arm was finally free, everything became faster and easier. In just a few minutes, Denis got himself out of his prison and I fell to my knees, completely spent.

We were alive, all three of us. Unscathed. Miracle men.

Cory didn't waste a second. He yelled, "Guys, get out, get going! Toward the valley! Fast. Now."

He was going in the wrong direction. Denis tried to shout out to him and so did I, but he had already taken off. In the meantime, I had clipped back in to one end of the rope with a carabiner. And thank goodness I had, because only a few strides into his "escape" valleyward, Cory suddenly disappeared into the void, taking a crazy flight into one of the biggest crevasses I'd ever seen. Denis and I felt the rope jerk in our harnesses and managed to arrest his fall.

"Cory! Cory! Coryyyy! Are you okay?"

"Yes!" His voice sounded hoarse from crying.

"Okay, take it easy. Do you have everything you need for climbing back up the rope?"

"Yes, yes. I have it all."

It took almost a quarter of an hour, but we finally saw him emerge from the crevasse.

"Come on, Cory, you can make it. Come toward us. Our backs are breaking!"

He took his first steps toward us and the rope slackened. It was a relief. I hugged him and calmed him, told him he was out of danger.

"Now tie in third. Denis and I will break trail. Go on. It'll be over soon."

The avalanche that had swept us away only moments before now became our path, and we walked along it quickly. We came to the opening of a couloir between two seracs and our flags came back into view. Like robots, we marched on, with Denis and I alternating leads. From then on, I had only one thought in my mind: get down, get down, and end this torture.

We were getting closer to the edge of the glacier. Only a few more steps and we would see the military camp, our salvation. Even though we knew a labyrinth of seracs riddled with crevasses lay ahead, it felt like we'd come to the end of a long tunnel, where hope became certainty.

We were sitting on the snow, looking below. Our goal was so close, but we were on empty. I got to my feet, took a few steps, and then dropped back down. Denis did the same, passing me. Just as he was about to sit down again he shouted, "Saeed Jan! Saeed Jaaaaan!"

"Simone! Saeed Jan and Hassan are just below us! They came to meet us! They broke trail!"

While I shouted out their names, Cory closed his eyes and collapsed backward onto the snow.

Somehow we all got back on our feet. With energy drawn from who knows where, we went to meet our two Pakistani angels. In a few minutes, we were all hugging one another. Hassan was crying. Saeed Jan pulled a bottle of cola and some cookies out of his pack, along with hot tea and some *ciapati* (the local flatbread).

Saeed Jan took my pack and Hassan took Cory's. Denis thanked them but declined, saying that at this point, with the trail already broken and him following at the back of the pack, it would be much easier to just keep carrying his own load for a few more minutes.

I remember walking as quickly as possible. Without a pack on, I felt like I was flying. Plus, I couldn't wait to get to base camp and cross the threshold of the mess tent, to feel alive once and for all, to feel safe, welcome, back at last.

I wasn't feeling anything, not fatigue, not pain, not joy. I had put everything on hold while I raced toward my objective. And then I found myself above the couloir in which our base camp was located. In an instant I was down. I turned toward the tents. I saw Didar coming toward me. I stopped because I wanted to truly enjoy that hug.

Five meters away from me, Didar spread his arms wide. I wasn't moving a muscle. I was smiling, waiting. When he reached me, I closed my eyes and squeezed him in the world's biggest, longest hug. And in that simple and sincere way, our magical, dramatic adventure came to a close.

AFTERWORD

NOW THAT THE BOOK IS finished, let me tell you how much I've enjoyed reliving my winter experiences with you. In order to write this book, I had to delve into a mind ill suited to storing memories and even less suited to recalling details. My mind has always been much more inclined to empty itself to make space for future adventures.

I've written of the cold, the wind and the snow, of bad weather and blizzards. I've written of great dreams and rude awakenings, of constructive criticism and gratuitous malice. I've written of friends, be they Nepali, Pakistani, or Kazakhstani. And all of this, right while I'm in the midst of yet another adventure.

The book you hold in your hands is the fruit of folly. Conceived and born from four little pages jotted while I was cozy at home with a never-ending list of things to do, this entire book was written in twenty days on Nanga Parbat, in winter, with frozen and gloved fingers and a hot-water bottle under the laptop to conserve the battery during the coldest hours of the day, or when the generator was off. It was written while I traveled from Milano to Islamabad or from Skardu to Gilgit, or during the three days of acclimatization. And the bulk of it was written right where I am writing this now—at base camp, while zipped into my sleeping bag and by the light of my headlamp, or sitting at the mess tent table between dumps of snow or between a nap and a meal.

Indeed, I never would have imagined writing a book on winter mountaineering while actually in the midst of an expedition, when the story of a past experience becomes an echo of the current one. I could almost say "never again!" but I can't complain. If I found myself writing in these conditions, it was so that I could be more faithful to my words. And I gave it my all, even when I feared it was almost impossible.

And there it is again, that same adjective: "impossible." But I wrote "almost" beside it—a small word that shifts the perspective, opens a window, gives you the sense that you can indeed change your life, and change the world.

Impossible. Unattainable. Pipe dream. Such labels have been applied to so many things. Yet history shows that those courageous enough to preface such labels with "almost" can accomplish amazing things and make a huge impact.

And so I conclude with this: Never believe in the existence of the impossible. May you find the inspiration and motivation to work ever harder at showing yourself, and the world, that the limits of what we can do, dream, and achieve are only ever inside ourselves. "Impossible" is an excuse for surrender.

APPENDIX 1

WINTER-ASCENT ATTEMPTS ON PAKISTANI 8000ERS

1987–1988, K2, *1st attempt*
Polish/British/Canadian expedition led by Andrzej Zawada
Altitude reached: 7300 meters

1988, BROAD PEAK, *1st attempt*
Polish expedition led by Maciej Berbeka
Foresummit reached: 8035 meters

1988–1989, NANGA PARBAT, *1st attempt*
Polish expedition led by Maciej Berbeka
Altitude reached: 6800 meters

1990–1991, NANGA PARBAT, *2nd attempt*
Polish expedition led by Maciej Berbeka
Altitude reached: 6600 meters

1996–1997, NANGA PARBAT, *3rd attempt*
Polish/Pakistani expedition led by Andrzej Zawada
Altitude reached: 7870 meters

1996–1997, NANGA PARBAT, *4th attempt*
British expedition led by Victor Saunders
Altitude reached: 6000 meters

1997–1998, NANGA PARBAT, *5th attempt*
Polish expedition led by Andrzej Zawada
Altitude reached: 6700 meters

2002–2003, K2, *2nd attempt*
International expedition led by Krzysztof Wielicki
Altitude reached: 7650 meters

2002–2003, BROAD PEAK, *2nd attempt*

Spanish/Italian expedition led by Juanito Oiarzabal
Altitude reached: 7000 meters

2004–2005, NANGA PARBAT, *6th attempt*

Austrian expedition led by Gerfried Goschl
Altitude reached: 6500 meters

2006–2007, NANGA PARBAT, *7th attempt*

Polish expedition led by Krzysztof Wielicki
Altitude reached: 6600 meters

2006–2007, BROAD PEAK, *3rd attempt*

Italian/Pakistani expedition led by Simone Moro
Altitude reached: 6800 meters

2007–2008, NANGA PARBAT, *8th attempt*

Italian/Pakistani expedition led by Simone La Terra
Altitude reached: 6000 meters

2007–2008, BROAD PEAK, *4th attempt*

Italian/Pakistani expedition led by Simone Moro
Altitude reached: 7800 meters

2008–2009, BROAD PEAK, *5th attempt*

Polish/Canadian expedition led by Artur Hajzer
Altitude reached: 7400 meters

2008–2009, NANGA PARBAT, *9th attempt*

Polish expedition led by Jacek Teler
Altitude reached: 5400 meters

2010–2011, BROAD PEAK, *6th attempt*

Polish expedition led by Artur Hajzer
Altitude reached: 7850 meters

2010–2011, GASHERBRUM I, *1st attempt*

Austrian/Canadian/Spanish expedition led by Gerfried Goschl
Altitude reached: 7100 meters

2010–2011, NANGA PARBAT, *10th attempt*

Polish expedition led by Tomasz Mackiewicz & Marek Klonowski
Altitude reached: 4860 meters

2010–2011, NANGA PARBAT, *11th attempt*

Russian expedition led by Sergey Tsygankov
Altitude reached: 3850 meters (did not reach base camp)

2010–2011, GASHERBRUM II, *1st attempt*

Italian/Kazakhstani/US expedition led by Simone Moro, first
winter ascent in the Karakoram
Altitude reached: 8035 meters

FIRST WINTER ASCENTS ON 8000ERS

February 17, 1980, EVEREST
Krzysztof Wielicki & Leszek Cichy (Polish)

January 12, 1984, MANASLU
Maciej Baebeka & Ryszard Gajewski (Polish)

January 21, 1984, DHAULAGIRI
Jerzy Kukuczka & Andrzej Czok (Polish)

February 12, 1985, CHO OYU
Maciej Baebeka & Maciej Pawlikowski (Polish)

January 11, 1986, KANGCHENJUNGA
Krzysztof Wielicki & Jerzy Kukuczka (Polish)

February 3, 1987, ANNAPURNA
Jerzy Kukuczka & Artur Haizer (Polish)

December 31, 1988, LHOTSE
Krzysztof Wielicki (Polish)

January 14, 2005, SHISHAPANGMA
Simone Moro & Piotr Morawsky (Italian/Polish)

February 9, 2009, MAKALU
Simone Moro & Denis Urubko (Italian/Kazakhstani)

February 2, 2011, GASHERBRUM II
Simone Moro, Denis Urubko, & Cory Richards (Italian/Kazakhstani/US)

SIMONE MORO'S CV

2012

- With Denis Urubko, Simone attempts the first winter ascent of Nanga Parbat (Himalaya, Pakistan, 8125 m). The expedition lasts fifty-one days and reaches 6600 meters before terrible weather conditions force them to turn back.

2011

- On February 2, Simone makes the first winter ascent of Gasherbrum II (Karakoram, 8035 m), with Denis Urubko and Cory Richards. With this exploit Simone makes history and becomes the first alpinist to reach three 8000-meter peaks during one winter season.
- He is among the nominees for the Piolet d'Or Asia 2011.
- He wins the Kolos prize in Poland.
- He wins the alpinism prize Società Alpinisti Tridentini.

2010

- Simone gets his license as a commercial helicopter pilot with an authorization to operate in Nepal.
- For the fourth time, he reaches the summit of Everest (Himalaya, 8848 m) via the south face, accomplishing the ascent and descent in forty-eight hours.
- In Stockholm he is named Explorer of the Year 2009.
- He is among the nominees for the Karl Unterkircher Award 2009.
- He receives the Eiger Award 2009.

2009

- Simone makes the first winter ascent of Makalu (Himalaya, 8462 m) with Denis Urubko. For twenty-nine years, great

climbers from all over the world had been attempting this record-breaking ascent.
- For this Makalu ascent, he is among the nominees for the Piolet d'Or Asia 2009.
- He receives the Dalla Longa prize.

2008

- Simone makes the first alpine-style ascent of Beka Brakai Chhok (Karakoram, 6940 m) in Pakistan, in forty-three hours. He is accompanied by Hervé Barmasse.
- For this Beka Brakai Chhok ascent he receives, once again, the Paolo Consiglio prize from the Italian Academic Alpine Club.
- Once more he attempts the winter ascent of Broad Peak (Karakoram, 8047 m), interrupted 200 meters from the summit.
- He receives the Dalla Longa prize.

2007

- Simone attempts the first winter ascent of Broad Peak (Karakoram, 8047 m), reaching 7200 meters twice, despite a monthlong storm.

2006

- Simone makes the first solo traverse of Everest from south to north (summit to base camp in four hours and thirty minutes).

2005

- Simone makes the first winter ascent of Shishapangma (Himalaya, 8013 m) via the Yugoslav route, a historic achievement.
- He opens a new route on Batokshi Peak (Pakistan, 6050 m).

2005 (CONTINUED)

- He attempts the winter ascent of Cerro Torre (Andes, 3102 m).

2004

- Simone attempts the first winter ascent of the south face along the Figueras route on Shishapangma (Himalaya, 8013 m), reaching just 300 meters short of the summit.
- He makes the first ascent of the north face of Khali Himal, also known as Baruntse North (Nepal, 7066 m).
- For this Khali Himal ascent, he wins the Russian Alpinism Championships—the first Westerner to do so—and receives the Paolo Consiglio prize from the Italian Academic Alpine Club.
- He attempts the ascent of Annapurna (Himalaya, 8091 m), interrupted 100 meters from the summit.

2003

- Simone is awarded the Pierre de Coubertin International Fair Play prize in Paris.
- In Italy he receives the Medaglia d'Oro al Valore Civile from President Ciampi.
- He opens a new route on Nanga Parbat at 2100 meters (Himalaya, Pakistan, 8125 m).
- He does the fast ascent of Broad Peak (Karakoram, 8047 m) in twenty-nine hours, and Mount Elbrus (Caucasus, 5642 m) in three hours and forty minutes.

2002

- Simone reaches the summit of Everest (Himalaya, 8848 m) for the second time.

- He does a fast ascent of Cho Oyu (Himalaya, 8201 m) in eleven hours.

2001

- Simone reaches the summit of Everest (Himalaya, 8848 m).
- The American Alpine Club confers on him the David A. Sowles Memorial Award.
- He makes the first winter ascent of Marble Wall (Tien Shan, 6400 m).
- Abandoning his climb he rescues, on his own, without oxygen, Tom Moores at an altitude of 8000 meters on Lhotse's west face.

1999

- In thirty-seven days Simone climbs Pik Lenin (7134 m), Pik Korjenevska (7105 m), Pik Komunism (7495 m), and Pik Khan Tengri (7010 m): he is the second man ever to have achieved this "alpine marathon."

1998

- Simone attempts Everest (Himalaya, 8848 m) along the north ridge, reaching 8200 meters before stopping due to avalanche danger.

1997

- The expedition on Annapurna (Himalaya, 8091 m), along the south face, is interrupted due to an avalanche at 6300 meters. Simone survives, but his two partners—Anatolij Boukreev and Dimitri Sobolev—are killed.
- He reaches the summit of Lhotse (Himalaya, 8516 m).
- He climbs icefalls graded ED (extremely difficult/M8).

1996

- Simone reaches the northwest summit of Shishapangma (Himalaya, 8013 m).
- He makes an attempt on Dhaulagiri (Himalaya, 8167 m), but is forced to stop at 7200 meters due to bad weather.
- He completes the fast ascent-descent of Fitz Roy (Andes, 3411 m) in twenty-five hours, climbing the west face.

1995

- Simone climbs Kangchenjunga (Himalaya, 8596 m), stopping at 7300 meters due to bad weather.

1994

- Simone makes a fast ascent of Lhotse (Himalaya, 8516 m), from 6300 meters in seventeen hours.
- He attempts an ascent of Shishapangma (Himalaya, 8013 m), stopping at 7400 meters due to avalanche danger.
- He climbs various routes in Italy up to grade 8b.

1993

- Simone makes a fast ascent of Aconcagua (Argentine Andes, 6962 m) in thirteen hours. He attempts the ascent of the south face, but stops at 6200 meters due to an avalanche.
- He opens a new winter route and quickly climbs the north face of Cerro Mirador (Chilean Andes, 6089 m), stopping 163 meters from the summit.
- He makes a solo ascent of Makalu (Himalaya, 8463 m) along the Kukuczka route.

1985–1992

- Simone makes his first expedition to Everest (Himalaya, 8848 m).
- He is part of the Italian Federation of Sports Climbing team and from 1987 to 1989 climbs more than thirty routes graded 8a and 8b+.

1980

- Simone starts his alpine career, first climbing in the mountains around Bergamo, then in the Dolomites.

ACKNOWLEDGMENTS

ALMOST EVERY SUCCESS IS THE result of teamwork. Sharing success is a cherished value of mine, one that tends to be neglected too often, whether in the realm of business or family or sport, or in society in general. We are always quick to take the credit but rarely take the blame.

There's no ghostwriter lurking behind this book. I wanted to write it myself. In so doing, I risked shooting myself in the foot because I only managed to submit it at the last second. But in the end, writing it gave me great satisfaction.

First, I want to thank those who bear the burden of sharing their lives with a man who is often—perhaps too often—far away. My wife, Barbara, and my son, Jonas, are certainly the ones who contribute the most to my happiness and the fulfillment of my dreams. It's a high price to pay, yet they never complain. My gratitude knows no bounds. And my other child, Martina, who has loved this father for twelve years, a father who has brought her joy, dreams, fun, and probably also great sadness—I would like her to be close by again and part of our serenity.

Thanks of a different kind goes to the one who kept me on a tight leash during this project. She prodded me continually and acted as liaison between me and the publisher, who would have preferred to get this manuscript in a somewhat less adventurous way. I'm speaking of Mariana Zanatta, my friend and witness at our wedding, my long-time climbing friend and colleague. She is what would be called my "manager," but our relationship is essentially one of sincere respect and pure friendship.

My third thank-you goes to many others:

To my mother and my brothers, who never asked me to quit. For thirty years, they have lived with fear in their hearts for this son and brother who spends so much of his life exposed to the undeniable dangers of the vertical world.

To Gianmario Besana, one of my best friends and an important touchstone. He lends perspective on the growth and development of how I represent and share my experiences.

To all of my sponsors, some of whom have been companions on my journey for thirty years now, who have never forced me to take risks or succeed at any cost and have always supported me. I want to mention Karl Heinz Salzburger in particular. Thirteen years ago, when he was head of The North Face, he made me part of the company's team. There, I found an organization capable of believing in and financing my dream of exploratory mountaineering. Thanks to him, I am still exploring today. Together with a large team, he and I keep the concept of "never stop exploring" alive. May you never stop exploring either, dear reader.

My final thanks go to Denis Urubko, my climbing partner during many of my most beautiful and prestigious experiences. I couldn't have found a better partner. I hope he can say the same of me.

Three days after finishing this book, I lost my friend, Mario Merelli. I'm sending him a special farewell on the cold air of Nanga Parbat. Ciao, Mario.

And finally, I must pay a very simple tribute to one last person: Thank you, Anatolij.

TRANSLATOR'S NOTE

IN JANUARY 2014, SIMONE MORO was on Nanga Parbat with David Göttler awaiting their summit window. Meanwhile, I was translating Simone's journal entries from his 2012 expedition on the same mountain. With Vancouver's winter skies drooping about my ears like a soggy toque, I followed Simone's crisp, high-alpine tweets and Facebook posts. I shared my translation journey on social media, too.

Translation is a peculiarly intimate act. When reading a book, especially a memoir, you enter into communion with the writer. Afterward, you feel as though you know them. Translating a book requires an even deeper, sustained immersion.

Technology in the wilderness can be a contentious subject, but Simone's posts from Nanga Parbat offered me a glimpse of how technology could add dimension to wilderness experience. I started to feel connected to this man whom I had never met and who was more than 6000 miles away. I also watched interviews and films to get a sense of how Simone sounded and moved. Added to the immediacy of his posts and photos, it was a recipe for a somewhat trippy experience. I felt at times like I was inhabiting him. Once or twice, I even had the impression (the delusion?) of glimpsing his essence.

This translation represents an ensemble of decisions, a dance of subjective and objective choices made with the aim of going beyond words to the deeper nuances. Together Simone's words formed an ocean into which I dove, seeking both content and identity. I hope I've surfaced with not only the meaning of his words, but also a glimmer of his spirit.

Monica Meneghetti
Vancouver, BC, June 2014

ABOUT THE AUTHOR

BORN IN 1967, SIMONE MORO has been climbing since the age of thirteen. His first major climb was a speed ascent of Aconcagua in winter (1993). He next made a speed ascent of Lhotse in 1994 (in the normal season). He has since gone on to reach the summits of Shishapangma, Makalu, and Gasherbrum II, all in winter. He has climbed in the Himalayas, Karakorum, Tian Shan, Pamir, Andes, Patagonia, and Antarctica, as well as in major ranges in Europe and North America. The recipient of numerous awards and honors for his climbing achievements, Simone is a popular speaker at the Banff Mountain Film and Book Festival. *The Call of the Ice* is his third book, and the first to be translated into English. He lives in Bergamo, Italy, with his wife, Barbara Zwerger, and two children.

OTHER TITLES YOU MIGHT ENJOY FROM MOUNTAINEERS BOOKS

Freedom Climbers: The Golden Age of Polish Climbing
Bernadette McDonald
"A brilliantly crafted tale of mountain and political adventure that reveals a golden era in Himalayan climbing that was as glorious as it was tragic."
–*Sir Chris Bonington*

Reinhold Messner: My Life at the Limit
Reinhold Messner
The most personal and reflective of all Reinhold Messner's books, this autobiography in interview format is updated through 2014 and has never before been published in English.

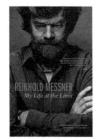

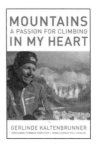

Mountains in My Heart:
A Passion for Climbing
Gerlinde Kaltenbrunner
Effusive, charismatic, and tough, Gerlinde Kaltenbrunner has climbed the fourteen 8000-meter peaks without supplemental oxygen or high-altitude porters.

Tilting At Mountains: Love, Tragedy, and Triumph on the World's Highest Mountains
Edurne Pasaban
The passionate and honest autobiography of the Basque woman who was the first woman to climb the fourteen 8000-meter peaks.

Psychovertical
Andy Kirkpatrick
Winner of the Boardman-Tasker Award with writing that, in the words of the prize judges, "grips the heart further and further."

www.mountaineersbooks.org